A Curious Student's Guide to the Book of Genesis

A Curious Student's Guide to the Book of Genesis

*Enduring Life Lessons
for the Twenty-First Century*

REUVEN TRAVIS

WIPF & STOCK · Eugene, Oregon

A CURIOUS STUDENT'S GUIDE TO THE BOOK OF GENESIS
Enduring Life Lessons for the Twenty-First Century

Copyright © 2020 Reuven Travis. All rights reserved. Except for brief quotations in critical publications or reviews, no part of this book may be reproduced in any manner without prior written permission from the publisher. Write: Permissions, Wipf and Stock Publishers, 199 W. 8th Ave., Suite 3, Eugene, OR 97401.

Illustrations by Eli Portman

Wipf & Stock
An Imprint of Wipf and Stock Publishers
199 W. 8th Ave., Suite 3
Eugene, OR 97401

www.wipfandstock.com

PAPERBACK ISBN: 978-1-7252-5692-7
HARDCOVER ISBN: 978-1-7252-5693-4
EBOOK ISBN: 978-1-7252-5694-1

Manufactured in the U.S.A. 06/17/20

In Honor of my Grandchildren
Matan Lev and Aiden Solomon Chiert
and
Aida Mae Levine

Millions saw the apple fall, but Newton asked why.
BERNARD BARUCH

Contents

Preface for Parents and Teachers	ix
Introduction	xv
Family Tree of the Book of Genesis	1
Bereshit—Let's Start at the Very Beginning	3
Noach—The Rains Come and Come and Come	13
Lech Lecha	
Part One—What It Means to Be Jewish	23
Part Two—The Story of Abraham and Sarah Begins	27
Vayera—Visitors and More Visitors	35
Chayei Sarah—Changes in the Family	45
Toldot—When Mom and Dad Can't Agree	53
Vayetze—Tricks and More Tricks	63
Vayishlach	
Part One—Do We Believe in Angels?	71
Part Two—Brothers Reunited	74
Vayeshev	
Part One—What's Up with the Joseph Story?	81
Part Two—The Long, Twisted Tale Begins	86
Miketz—One Dream or Two?	93
Vayigash—Long Time No See	101
Vayechi—All Good Things Come to an End	109
About the Author	115

Preface for Parents and Teachers

I have been an educator for more than twenty years, and in that time, I have taught the book of Genesis to students from second grade through high school. As you can imagine, the stories, imagery, and commentaries I used in teaching small children differed greatly from those I employed when teaching high school seniors. In reflecting on this, I am often reminded of an insight I once heard from Rabbi Berel Wein. What is the difference, he asked in a lecture, between teaching a subject such as math and teaching Torah (also called the "Five Books of Moses" or the "Pentateuch")? In a math class, once a student learns that two plus two equals four, he or she need not revisit or relearn this fact. However, with Torah, which Jews read each week in synagogues around the world, the same chapters are studied by everyone—the second grader, the middle school student, the high schooler, and their teachers—and the Jewish people do so week after week, year after year.

The hope is that each student of Torah, regardless of his or her age, gains new insights each time the text is relearned.

These new learnings notwithstanding, it is important to teach the section of the Torah read each week in synagogues in an age-appropriate manner and context. When teaching children, which is the goal of this book, this means picking and choosing among the Torah's many lessons so as to emphasize those that these young students can grasp and appreciate. For example, this book does not discuss the story of Cain and Abel—not because it is unimportant but because it is simply too difficult to teach and discuss fratricide with third-, fourth-, and fifth-grade students. The same is true for the story of Dinah and for the encounter between Judah and Tamar.

Another important aspect of teaching young students is the importance of helping them understand the difference between text and midrash (a form of biblical exegesis developed and employed by ancient Judaic authorities that remains to this day an important tool for discerning the meaning of the Torah). Midrash provides us with important insights into the text and offers interesting backstories, but students should never conflate it with the biblical text itself. The text is the text, and midrash is commentary on the text.

When using midrash to make the text easier to understand,[1] I have always been guided by the approach of Rabbi Moshe ben Nachman, the great biblical commentator from the 1200s. In his famous disputation with the apostate Jew Pablo Christiani, Rabbi Moshe made this observation:

> We possess three genres of literature. The first is the Bible or Tanakh, and all of us believe in its words with a complete trust. The second is the Talmud, and it is an exposition of the commandments of the Torah, for the Torah contains 613 commandments. Not a single one of them is left unexplained by the Talmud. We believe in the Talmud with respect to its exposition of the commandments. The third type of book that we possess is the Midrash, and it is like sermons . . . concerning this collection, for one who believes it, good. For one who does not believe it, there is no harm. . .[2]

I have never been one to insist that students see midrashic expositions as accurate, historical accounts, nor have I framed midrashic stories as mere parables. How a student chooses to see this literature is up to him or her. What cannot be ignored or diminished are the important lessons the midrash offers us. For instance, it

---

1. When I use midrash to explain a text or story, which I will do on occasion, I will identify it as such or refer to it as "the rabbinic tradition."

2. Ramban (Nahmanides), *The Disputation at Barcelona*, trans. Charles B. Chavel (New York: Shilo, 1983), paragraph 39.

does not matter to me whether the large idol in Terach's shop actually grabbed a stick and smashed all the others in a jealous rage or whether the midrash uses this as a literary tool to make its point. The power of Abraham's question to his father—Why do you worship this idol as a god if you don't believe it could smash all the other idols?—endures. It shows us that even a child can see the foolishness of worshipping man-made figures of stone.

An important note on the methodology I use to present and examine the central stories of Genesis is in order. Most students of the Bible are familiar with its system of chapters and verse numbers. This division, which has been universally adopted, was first made in the Latin Bible in the thirteenth century, most likely by Stephen Langston.[3] Langston's system was consequently employed in the concordances of the Vulgate, and this in turn gave Rabbi Isaac Nathan[4] the idea for the first Hebrew concordance. The citations in this concordance first give the number of the Vulgate chapter and then give the number of the masoretic[5] verse, which remains to this day the standard format of the printed Hebrew Bible.

Yet the printed format of the Hebrew Bible is not the one used for ritual purposes. As part of Jewish prayer services on the Sabbath, different portions of the Torah are read each week.[6] These readings are commonly referred to as the weekly *parasha* or *sedra*. The starting and ending points of each *parasha* have nothing at all

---

3. Stephen Langton was an English cardinal of the Roman Catholic Church and Archbishop of Canterbury between 1207 and his death in 1228. The dispute between King John of England and Pope Innocent III over his election as archbishop was a major factor in the crisis that produced the Magna Carta in 1215.

4. Rabbi Isaac Nathan ben Kalonymus was a French Jewish philosopher who lived in the fourteenth and fifteenth centuries. In the introduction to his concordance, Rabbi Isaac wrote that he was completely ignorant of the Bible until his fifteenth year. Prior to that time, his studies had been restricted to the Talmud and religious philosophy.

5. In rabbinic Judaism, the Masoretic Text is the authoritative Hebrew and Aramaic text of the Bible. It was primarily copied, edited, and distributed by a group of Jews known as the Masoretes between the seventh and tenth centuries CE.

6. There are fifty-four such weekly portions, which means that a double portion is read on some weeks.

to do with Langston's system for organizing the Bible. Rather, they reflect the long-standing masoretic tradition.

Given my background and training as an Orthodox Jewish rabbi and educator, it made sense for me to organize this book according to these weekly *parashas*. It is a system I know well and am comfortable with. More importantly, these weekly readings, in my opinion, present a more logical flow for the major themes and stories of Genesis than do the chapter and verse numbers in common usage.[7]

Each chapter of this book will open with a brief overview and synopsis of the weekly Torah reading. Then will come a section I call "Life Lessons from This Week's Reading," which has the goal of helping young students think more deeply about the text read each week, as opposed to merely memorizing certain incidents from the narrative. Finally, there will be questions for students to think about as they begin to make the lessons from each week's reading their own.

All translations of biblical verses in this book are from *Tanakh: A New Translation of the Holy Scriptures according to the Traditional Hebrew Text* (Philadelphia: Jewish Publication Society, 1985) unless otherwise indicated. This translation is available in the public domain and with a free public license thanks to Sefaria (www.sefaria.org), a nonprofit organization that, in its own words, is dedicated to assembling "a free, living library of Jewish texts."

In closing, I would like to thank my dear friend and colleague Lisa Marks. Lisa is a gifted and passionate educator with whom I have worked for many years. She is the type of teacher adults wish they had had as children and are grateful for when their children end up in her class. Lisa gave me thoughtful and productive feedback as I was writing this book, and the end product was much improved due to her suggestions and insights.

---

7. Indeed, there are many chapter breaks that interrupt the logical flow of the narrative, something the masoretic tradition avoids. Look, for example, at the end of chapter 43 of Genesis and the beginning for chapter 44. This is clearly a single narrative, one we will discuss in great detail later in this book, and most modern editors would be confounded by the insertion of a new chapter here.

Preface for Parents and Teachers

I would also like to thank my daughter Rachel Travis. Rachel has an odd notion that she owes me for having read and edited just about every paper she wrote in high school, in college (as a Judaic studies major), and throughout graduate school (at least when she was pursuing a master's degree in Jewish culture and visual arts—her mother, a Senior VP with an MBA at one of the country's largest banks, handled the editing chores when Rachel went on to get an MBA). This is my fourth book, and Rachel has read them all, from the earliest (and roughest) drafts to the final manuscripts. If none of these books had been published and our collaboration was the only outcome of the process, that alone would have made each project worthwhile.

I would be remiss if I did not thank the fine folks at Wipf & Stock. I was amazed and thrilled when they agreed to publish my first book, on the book of Job, and even more so when they accepted the second, on the book of Numbers, for publication. While my amazement fades just a little with each subsequent manuscript they accept, my gratitude does not.

Rabbi Reuven Travis

Introduction

The Torah, given many, many years ago by God, is a very special book. Here's why.

First, it tells us clearly about things in life that we should do or that we should avoid. (We call these "commandments," or *mitzvot* in Hebrew.) It's not that God is being bossy. Instead, He wants us to be truly good people, and the Torah teaches us how to be kind, how to care for the sick, how to care for people who don't have enough money to feed themselves or their children, how to always be honest and fair, how to respect our parents and teachers. But it is important to know that while God gives us these lessons and commandments, He wants us to decide for ourselves whether we follow them and whether we turn out to be really good people or not. God wants this for us. He hopes that we will turn out to be good people, but He trusts us enough to let us decide.

Second, the Torah is filled with amazing stories. Some are stories of brave men and women doing incredible things, but there are also stories that tell us of people just living their lives. Sometimes the most valuable and the most powerful lessons we can learn from the Torah come from people's daily lives: how they speak to their husbands and wives, how they treat their children, how they interact with their neighbors, how they make really hard decisions.

Finally, and perhaps most important, the Torah teaches us to ask questions. Why would Adam and Eve eat from the one tree God told them not to eat from? Why would the people try to build a tower that reached the heavens? What made Noah so special that only he (along with his family) was spared from the great flood? Sometimes the answers to our questions are very clear from the text of the Torah. Sometimes it seems like the answers we seek are hidden away, and so we are left to think and wonder.

It is a good skill to learn to ask good questions, even if we don't get good answers to our good questions. In fact, our questions are often better than the answers we get! Asking questions can make us smarter (or at least more knowledgeable). Asking questions can also deepen our connections to the ones we ask, whether we are asking our parents, our teachers, or even God. And at the end of the day, that is a major reason for us to study the Torah and to follow its lessons. By doing so, we not only become better people, but we grow closer to God.

With this in mind, let's begin our studies with the Torah's most amazing story, that of creation.

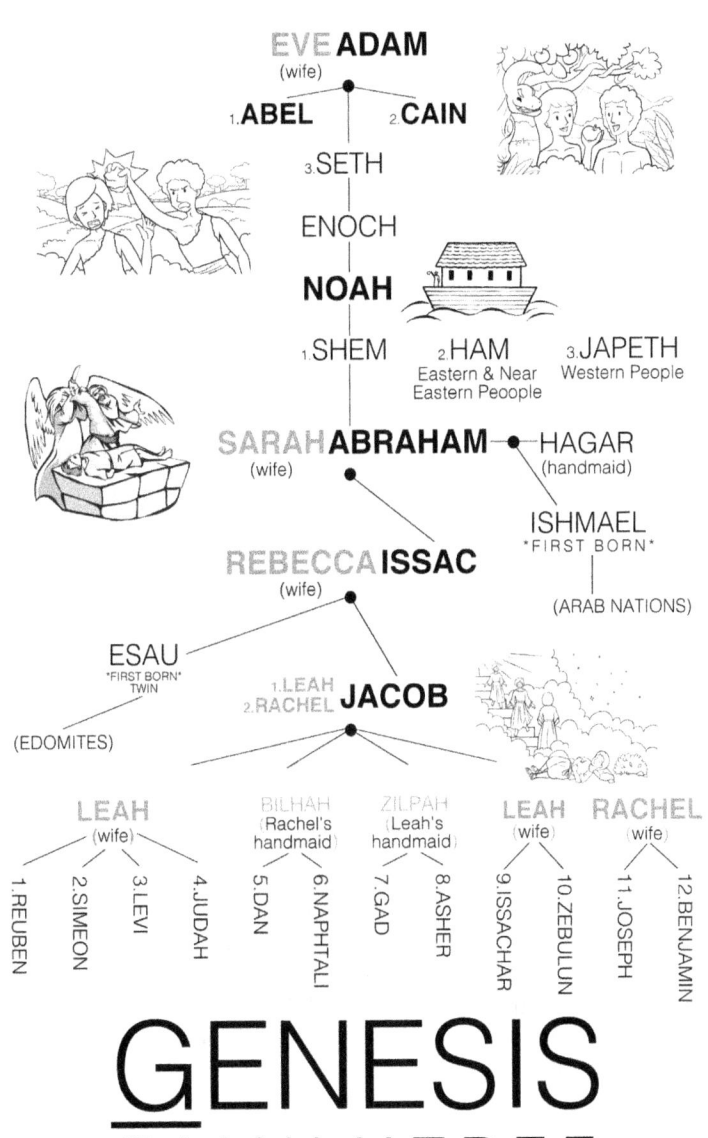

GENESIS
FAMILY TREE

Bereshit

(Gen 1:1–6:8)

LET'S START AT THE VERY BEGINNING

Summary of This Week's Reading

Bereshit tells us about the creation of the world. The first thing God does is create all the material He needs to build the heavens and the earth. (One way to think of this is that God makes something like LEGO® pieces that He then puts together on each day of creation to form new stuff.) Each day, for six days, He puts things together—things like the sun, moon, and stars as well as the oceans and dry land. He then forms all kinds of living creatures: birds in the sky, fish and other sea creatures in the oceans, and many different wild animals that roam the dry land. The only new things God creates (rather than just assembling them from the material He made before) are the "great sea monsters" that He creates on day five and humans, whom He creates on day six. At the end of the sixth day, God stops building and assembling things. On the seventh day, He rests, and by doing so, He gives us the whole idea of the Sabbath.

When God creates the first person, Adam, He forms his body from the dust of the earth. God then blows the breath of life into his nostrils, and Adam becomes a living being. At first, Adam is alone, unlike every other living creature, but God decides that it is not good for him to be alone. So God creates the first woman, whom Adam calls Eve, and they become husband and wife.

After they are married, God puts them in the Garden of Eden to live. They can do as they please and are to work the garden. The only thing they cannot do is eat the fruit from the "Tree of Knowledge of Good and Evil."

In the garden with them is a serpent, who tricks Eve into eating the forbidden fruit. She shares the forbidden fruit with Adam. Because they did not listen to this one command, God makes them leave the garden.

After leaving the garden, Adam and Eve have two sons, Cain and Abel. Cain decides to give a present to God, something we call a "sacrifice." Abel thinks this is such a good idea that he also gives one to God. Looking at both gifts (the fruits Cain found growing from the ground and the animals Abel himself raised), God decides that Abel's is nicer. This makes Cain so angry and so jealous that he kills his brother Abel.

This sad story is not the end of this week's reading. It goes on to tell us that Adam and Eve have a third son, Seth, and that from Seth's family comes Noah, whose story we will read about in our next chapter.

Life Lessons from Bereshit

The first of the Torah's weekly readings, *Bereshit*, has many important stories that are familiar to many people. It also makes us ask some very important questions about how we learn Torah and how we should live our lives.

Ready to get started? Good.

Creation Facts or Creation Story?

Not surprisingly, the Torah begins with the story of creation. This makes sense. After all, much of the Torah is intended to teach us about life and our place in the world. Why not start with how the world (and all of us!) came to be?

As you read through the opening verses of *Bereshit* and its description of creation, you can't help but wonder: How did this all work? Scientists have been asking this question for hundreds of years, and today, the most widely accepted explanation of how the universe began is something called the "big bang theory." Its name describes it very well. Scientists believe that the universe as we know it started with what they call a "small singularity." (Scientists may understand what this means, but most of us don't!) Non-scientists like to think of the universe as starting with a "big bang." This means that all the parts of our universe—atoms, energy, everything—simply came into being in an instant. BANG! Just like that.

This big bang theory is not news to the Jewish people. The rabbis and Jewish sages were discussing and writing about this idea as early as the time of the Talmud. They believe that the very first verse of the Torah teaches us that God created everything from nothing (*yesh me-ayin* in Hebrew).

Still, this does not answer our question about how this all really happened. The Torah tells us that God spoke ten times to create the universe. For example, "God said, 'Let there be light'; and there was light."

Got it now? Probably not, and not even the greatest Torah scholars or the most brilliant scientists can explain how exactly creation happened from verses like this. So what are the opening verses of the Torah trying to teach us?

First, the Torah is telling us that there are some things in the world, maybe even many things, that we humans cannot understand. We believe that God created our world, but the exact details are too hard for us to fully understand. Scientists have ideas about how creation actually happened, but they don't know for sure. Jewish thinkers have tried to understand why God created the world, and they have no good answers, either. Accepting that there are things in life we cannot explain or understand helps us to be more accepting of life and happier in the lives we lead. This does not mean that we should stop asking questions. We should simply stop expecting answers to all our questions.

Second, these verses make clear that the Torah was written for people in a way we can understand. This is why many Jewish scholars and teachers see the beginning of *Bereshit* as a story full of important lessons. They believe that *Bereshit* should not be read literally (Again, what does "let there be light" really mean? How exactly did the light come into existence?) but rather as a story written in a way that people can learn from.

Now, there are some people who insist that the creation story must be true and that it happened exactly as it is written in the Torah. But the better way to read it, according to many Jewish thinkers and teachers, is as a story meant to teach us certain lessons. Here is another reason why this is so.

Bereshit tells us that God created the universe in six days and rested on the seventh, which is why we have the Sabbath (and the Sabbath is one of the most important parts of the creation story). But if you read the story very carefully, you will see that the sun and moon do not appear until day four. How can days be counted without a sun and a moon? Maybe the Torah is teaching us that creation took place in six steps or stages, and it is just using the word "day" so that we understand that each step had a beginning and an end, just as a day does.

> *Can you think of something that happened in your life that actually taught you an important lesson? Do you have a favorite story or book that also taught you an important lesson? Do you think it makes a difference whether you learn a lesson from real life or from a book or story?*

What Came First, and Why Does It Matter, Anyway?

Whether you like to think of creation as taking place in six steps or six days, the chart below summarizes how creation unfolded.

Bereshit (Gen 1:1–6:8)

STEP (OR DAY)	WHAT CAME INTO BEING
One	The first thing God does is create all the material He needs to assemble the heavens and the earth. (One way to think of this is that God made something like LEGO® pieces that He then put together on each day of creation to form new stuff.) Using this material, God forms light and then separates light and darkness.
Two	God next puts together the heavens and separates them from the world below. At this point, the world below the heavens is completely covered in water.
Three	God gathers all the water below the heavens into one area. He does this so that dry land can be seen. He calls these waters "seas," and He calls the dry land "earth." He then decides that the dry land should be covered with grasses and plants and trees of every kind, including fruit trees.
Four	God next assembles the sun, moon, and stars. This means that there is now an idea of "day" (when the sun is out) and "night" (when the moon and stars are out).
Five	Now that there are dry land and oceans, God wants to fill them with living creatures. He forms birds of all kinds and sea creatures of all kinds. And instead of using His creation LEGOs®, He then *creates* something completely new: the great sea monsters. (To be honest, we aren't exactly sure what these great sea monsters were.)
Six	Having formed birds and sea creatures, God turns His attention to the dry land. He begins by forming all kinds of land animals, from cows to snakes and snails to wild animals of every kind. What's left? Humans, and these God *creates* in His own image. (This does not mean that we look like God or that He looks like us. It means that like God, we have the ability to make decisions for ourselves.)
Seven	God's work of creation is all done. He stops working and rests. (How exactly God "rests" is a very, very good question.) He calls this "day" the Sabbath, and He blesses it and says that it should be a holy time.

Look at the chart again. What do you notice about creation? That the simpler forms of life come first.[1] These simple things include plants and trees. Then come birds and sea creatures, followed by all the animals that live on dry land. Only in the end does God create humans.

---

1. Even people who do not believe that God created the world and instead think that evolution explains it all agree that the order in which life appeared on earth is more or less as the first chapter of Genesis describes it.

This is interesting. God makes it clear that humans are to be in control of how most things go on our planet. Why, then, does God create people last and not first? Wouldn't it make sense to begin with the most important thing and work your way backward from there?

The rabbis thought of this question long before we did, and they see in the order of creation an important lesson about how we should see ourselves and how we should understand our role in the world. They remind us (in a book called *Bereshit Rabba*) that even things we see as completely unimportant, like fleas or mosquitos or flies, were all created before humans. It is as if God were saying, "Listen, bigshot. I made fleas and mosquitos and flies before you. What makes you think you're so very important?" This teaches us not to have a big ego—not to think that we're better or more important than others.

> *Have you ever had a friend who acted like he or she was better or more important than you? How did that make you feel? What do you think you could have done to let him or her know that everyone is important in some way?*

When Even One Rule is One Too Many

Let's assume that the first humans, Adam and Eve, understand the lesson of the flea, mosquito, and fly and understand their role in this world. God puts them in a very special place, the Garden of Eden. He tells them that they are to take care of the garden. And they have only one rule to follow: eat anything you want that you find in the garden except for the fruit from the Tree of Knowledge of Good and Bad.[2]

What could be better than living in paradise with almost no rules to follow? In fact, you may be asking why God gives Adam and Eve any rules at all. The answer is simple. People are not machines. They are not programmed to do one thing or the other. People make choices all the time about what they should or should

---

2. Despite the many illustrations and paintings that have been done over time showing this tree to be an apple tree, it most certainly was *not* an apple tree. Most Jewish sources believe it was a fig tree. Why? Because when Adam and Eve first realize that they need something to cover up their nakedness, they grab the closest thing to them—fig leaves.

not do. That's how people learn and grow, and that is what God wants from Adam and Eve: for them to learn and grow, even if that means they will sometimes make bad choices.

And, boy, do they make a bad choice! They do the one thing God tells them *not* to do: eat from the Tree of Knowledge of Good and Bad.

Why God tells them not to eat from this tree isn't so important. What matters is that He gives them one rule to follow, and He tells them what will happen if they break this rule: "as soon as you eat of it, you shall die." (As we all know, they do not die after eating the fruit, but we'll get to that later.)

So, what happens? And what are we to learn from this story? The first lesson has to do with jealousy and the bad things that can happen when a person is jealous of something his or her friend has.

In the garden with Adam and Eve is a snake, but not any old snake. As the text tells us, this one can walk and talk and is really, really smart. (By the way, this walking, talking snake is another reason many Jewish scholars and teachers think *Bereshit* should be read as a story and not as something that actually happened.) The midrash tells us even more, and we turn to it because this is a very complicated story. According to the midrash, the snake is also jealous. He loves Eve and wants to be with her. He thinks that a snake and a woman may be able to live happily ever after. But there's a big problem, and his name is Adam. Eve loves Adam and doesn't want to be with the snake, so the snake wants revenge. His jealousy makes him want to trick Eve into breaking the one rule God gave her and Adam.

How is he able to do this? Because Adam makes a mistake, and he doesn't even know he's making it. He is just trying to be extra careful. You see, God tells Adam, and only Adam, not to eat from the fruit from the tree. It is Adam's job to share this warning with Eve, and to make sure she'll be really careful, Adam adds to God's warning. God only says not to eat from the tree. Adam tells Eve that they are not to eat from the tree *or even touch it*. After all, if you don't touch the tree, you can never eat its fruit.

Somehow, the snake knows about Adam's warning to Eve. One day, he is talking with her as they stand near the Tree of Knowledge of Good and Bad. He asks Eve, "Did God really tell you not to eat from this tree?"

"Yes, He did," answers Eve, "and what's more, He told us not to even touch it." Here is the opening the snake is looking for. Here is how he will get his revenge. He trips Eve. She stumbles, and to regain her balance, she grabs onto the tree. Yes, *that* tree. The Torah tells us what happens next. To her great surprise, she does not die, as Adam had told her would happen if she touched the tree. What's more, it is as if Eve were seeing the tree for the first time. And what does she see? She sees that the fruit is very, very beautiful and looks delicious. What's more, she convinces herself that eating the fruit will make her very smart—maybe even as smart as God!

Let's be clear. Adam means well, but he is not careful with his words. He should have shared with Eve exactly what God told him. By adding to the words of God and telling Eve she should not even touch the tree, Adam makes it possible for the snake to trick her. This is the second important lesson we learn from this story: to be very careful with the things we say.

> *Have you ever been less than careful with the words you use, and as a result, a friend got upset with you or your parents became angry with you? Did this make you stop and think of a better way you could have said things? Did it help you become more careful with your words?*

Getting into Trouble is No Fun, Especially by Yourself

As soon as Eve eats from the tree, she knows she made a mistake. What does she do next? She brings the fruit to Adam to share it with him. Oh, my goodness, why? And why does Adam eat the fruit? Here we have the third important lesson this story comes to teach us: that things happen because of our actions and that if those things are bad, we must be willing to say, "I did this" or "it was my fault."

Eve is scared. She has broken the one rule God gave her. And like many of us, she thinks it will be less scary if there is someone to share this with. She isn't thinking about what is going to happen because of what she does. She isn't ready to say, "I made a mistake." It seems like she is just looking for someone to share her punishment!

It would be easy to judge Eve, but that isn't what the story is trying to teach us here. Eve has what we could call a very human reaction to her wrongdoing. In time, both she and Adam will feel bad about breaking this rule, and in time, they will repent and try to find a way to make up with God. But in the moment, her fear and her embarrassment are too strong, and rather than admit her mistake, she wants someone else to take part in her bad choice.

As for Adam, he now has to make a choice of his own. Will he follow the rule of God and not eat the fruit? If he does, he will lose Eve, because God tells him that he will die on the day that he (or she) eats the fruit from the tree. If he ignores the rule and eats the fruit, he, Adam, will be with Eve. Maybe they will die together, or maybe, just maybe, God will be merciful and give them a different punishment (which is exactly what He does).

Unlike Eve, Adam does not try to ignore or forget what he does. He just thinks that breaking the rule is worth the punishment. People often do this. They break rules and do things they shouldn't, knowing full well that there will consequences: time out, being grounded, having your internet access taken away from you, or, in the case of Adam and Eve, being sent out of the garden forever. And maybe this is the point of the story.

God does not want to punish people. He prefers that we make good choices, but He is prepared to let us make bad ones, even when we know (or think we know) what the punishment will be. God's biggest hope is that we will learn from our mistakes and not repeat them in the future. This is why the story of Adam, Eve, and the snake is so important and why God includes it in this week's Torah reading. He wants us to understand that bad choices have consequences and that we should be careful about this. We don't always know how these consequences will work out, but we need to know that they will be there, waiting to happen, whether for good or for bad.

> *Did you ever do something wrong and then try to get someone else in trouble, like Eve did? How did that work out in the end? How did it make the other person feel?*

Noach

(Gen 6:9–11:32)

THE RAINS COME AND COME AND COME

Summary of This Week's Reading

We are introduced in this week's reading to a world of violence. A world so violent that it makes God regret ever having created the world. But rather than destroying everything and starting over with something completely new, God finds one person, Noah, worth saving. God speaks to Noah and tells him to build a large wooden boat. (We call this boat "the ark" or sometimes "Noah's ark.") It takes Noah a very long time to build the ark, and when it's done, God has two of every kind of animal (male and female) come to Noah to go inside his ark.

Once the animals and Noah's family (his wife, his three sons, and their wives) are safely inside the ark, it begins to rain. It rains without a break for 40 days and 40 nights. It rains so much that even the highest mountains on earth are covered by water. When the rain stops, the waters covering the earth toss and turn for 150 more days. Only then do the waters begin to shrink away.

The waters go down enough that the ark comes to rest on top of a mountain, Mount Ararat. But there is still water as far as Noah can see. He sends out a series of birds—first a raven and then doves—to see if they can find dry land anywhere. When the last dove Noah sends out does not come back, Noah knows that he and his family and all the animals can leave the ark. And they are certainly ready to leave, because it's been a whole year since the rains first began to fall!

When Noah leaves the ark, he understands that he and his family must rebuild the world, and the first step is to thank God for saving him and his family. Noah builds an altar and offers sacrifices to God (just like Cain and Abel did). God accepts these sacrifices and promises to never again destroy the world. He then tells Noah the rainbow will be a sign of this promise and of God's renewed connection with humankind. God also gives Noah a few commandments to keep, like not to kill and not to steal.

Noah's descendants, that is, his grandchildren and great grandchildren and so on, remain together for a long time. They all speak the same language. They all wear similar clothes. They all have the same customs. And then they decide to build a tower that reaches the heavens to show how great and powerful they are. This disappoints and angers God, and He now sees that Noah's descendants must be separated. To do this, God makes all the people speak new languages, and since they cannot understand each other, each group of people with the same language moves far away, so that they end up in different places around the world.

This week's reading concludes by briefly telling us about the ten generations of people who lived from the time of Noah until the time of Abram (who is later given the name "Abraham" by God).

Life Lessons from Noach

At some point, you probably heard something about Noah and the great flood, or about his ark and how the animals came to the ark two by two. But there is much more to the story than this, as we will soon see.

Noach (Gen 6:9–11:32)

Growing Confused About God

While *Noach* is very much about the flood and Noah himself, the first lesson it teaches us is about God. However, to really understand this lesson, we must first take a look at the people who lived at the time of the story. The Torah isn't clear about the details of what exactly people were doing in those days, but what they were doing wasn't good. In fact, it was so bad that the Torah uses words like "wicked" and "lawless" to describe the people's actions. Plus, it tells us that they were doing "evil all the time!"

Before we try to figure out what this "evil" that people were doing all the time is, we need to think about how they came to do such evil. What happened to their connection with God?

Although only ten generations have passed from the time when Adam and Eve knew God and spoke with Him, people pretty much ignore God by the time Noah is born. Instead, as the midrash teaches us, people think they can honor God simply by respecting and even worshipping His great creations, such as the sun and the moon.

It's easy to see how they make this mistake. Imagine that the president wanted to visit your school, but his schedule was very full. He just couldn't find the time to come himself, so he decided to send one of his important assistants, like the vice president. The students would be disappointed that the president himself couldn't visit them, but they would be very respectful to the person the president sent in his place. They would treat this person just as they would treat the president.

This is what happens from the time Adam and Eve are created until the time Noah is born. People treat the sun and the moon just like they would treat God. After all, they can see the sun and the moon. They can watch them appear day in and day out. But while we believe that God is everywhere, we cannot see Him or feel Him or hear Him. It's not so hard to understand how people back then got confused and focused on the visible, like the sun and the moon, while forgetting the God they couldn't see. And as we will see, bad things happen when people forget about God.

How Things Could Get Worse

Of course, this makes God sad, but not angry enough to destroy the world with a flood. What is it, then, that God thinks is worse than worshipping things like the sun and moon as if they were gods? To answer this, we need to look carefully at the words the Torah uses to describe the actions of the people. One word in particular is very important.

The Torah uses the world "lawlessness" in describing what the people are doing. The Hebrew word for "lawlessness" is *chamas*. Yes, this word is used for describing how people break or ignore the law, but it means something else, too. It means to break the law violently.

How do the people of Noah's time break the law violently? Think about a thief. He can sneak into a store or someone's home late at night, when he knows that they will be away or asleep. He sneaks in and out quietly, because he doesn't want to get caught and he doesn't want to hurt anyone. He is breaking the law, but with no violence.

Now imagine that he does not care if he gets caught or if he hurts someone else. Instead of sneaking into a store, he instead stops people on the street, threatens to beat them up, and demands their money. If they say no, he will hurt them to get want he wants. This is breaking the law violently.

Violent people don't care about other people or help other people. And when people don't care about one another, bad things usually happen.

This kind of violence, not caring whether other people get hurt, that makes God decide it's time to destroy the world.

> *How often do you help others, whether it's at home or at school? Do you think it's important to help other people? Why? And in what ways does this show that you care about them?*

It's About Second Chances

Right now, you should be thinking, "Wait a minute. God brings a flood, but He doesn't destroy the world." Good for you, because that's right. God is upset. God is sad. Yet He doesn't do a complete reboot. He doesn't create Adam and Eve 2.0. Even when people make bad choices—even when they make choices so bad that they make God sad or angry—He is ready to forgive them and give them another chance. That is what God does. That is what God wants to do. That is the very important lesson we learn about God from the story of the flood.

The question we need to ask now is this: What did Noah do to get a second chance? What made him so different from everyone else that God wanted to save him and his entire family? In answering these questions, we will learn another important lesson from this week's Torah reading, only this time it is a lesson about people and not about the ways of God.

> *Have you ever made a bad choice and done something you shouldn't have, but then your parents or teachers gave you another chance? Why do you think they did this?*

Different Ways of Being Good

What do we know about Noah? We know that he's 500 years old when he begins having children. We also know that he "found favor with the Lord," although we aren't quite sure what it means to "find favor" in God's eyes.[1] Most important, Noah is described in the Torah as a very righteous man who walks with God. Wow! Noah must have been really special to receive such compliments.

Noah is certainly a very special person, and even if the Torah doesn't tell us exactly what makes him so special, one thing is clear. Of all the great men and women mentioned in the Torah, only Noah is described as "righteous" and "blameless."

---

1. Some of the scholars and rabbis we rely on to help us understand difficult words in the Torah think that Noah "found favor" in the eyes of God because everything he did was pleasing and sweet to God. The Torah tells us this, that he found favor, to compare Noah's pleasing deeds to the wicked and violent actions of the other people of his generation.

Given this, Noah should be a role model to all of us when we think about working hard to become better people and becoming the best versions of ourselves that we can.

All of us today can trace our family trees back to Noah, because it is he and his family who rebuild the world after the flood. In a way, like Adam and Eve before him, Noah is one of the fathers of humanity. But for all his greatness, Noah is not the first Jew. As we will read next week, that honor belongs to Abraham. Why is this? Why was Noah special enough to be an ancestor to us all but not special enough to be the first Jew?

The answer is simple. Noah works hard at being a good person and at only doing the right thing, and he does this at a time when everyone else is doing bad and violent things. No one could blame Noah for thinking that the people around him couldn't change their ways and that it would be a waste of time for him to even try to get them to change. Instead, it's as if Noah says, "It doesn't matter what other people do. I am going to do the right thing, always." In fact, when God appears to Noah and tells him about His plan to flood the world, Noah listens very carefully to God's instructions on how to build the ark: how big it should be, what kind of wood it should be made of, how many of each animal to bring into it.[2] He doesn't argue with God and try to get Him to change His mind about destroying the world.

We will look at the story more closely when we get to *Vayera* (Gen 18:1–22:24), but know that when God decides to destroy the towns of Sodom and Gomorrah and tells Abraham about His plans, Abraham argues and argues and argues to try and get God to spare the two towns. What can we learn from this?

Noah teaches us how to be "righteous" and "blameless," and these are good things. However, it is Abraham who teaches us a different way to be righteous, and it involves always caring for others. This character trait of always caring for others is one of the things that defines the Jewish people.

---

2. While most of the animals came in pairs of males and females, some were brought in in groups of seven. Noah uses animals from these groups of seven to offer sacrifices to God once the flood is over and he and his family are safe.

NOACH (GEN 6:9–11:32)

We're People, Not Angels (or Even Machines)

There is another important lesson about people in *Noach*. What does it mean to be human? It depends on whom you ask. It could mean being able to communicate using words, symbols, or even funny faces. It could also mean being able to make our own decisions and then accept the consequences of them. It might even mean being able to think about the past, present, and future.

One thing it does not mean is being perfect.

Unlike other cultures or religions that often think their founders were perfect or were like supermen and superwomen, the Jewish people see the patriarchs (Abraham, Isaac, and Jacob) and the matriarchs (Sarah, Rebekah, Rachel, and Leah) as people—very special and very great people, but still, only people. This means that they sometimes get mad or jealous and that they sometimes make wrong choices. That is what people do, because we aren't angels. We aren't machines. We aren't perfect, and neither were the men and women who were the founders of the Jewish people. But the patriarchs and matriarchs always did good. They always tried to help others. They always tried to act in a way that made God happy and proud of them.

Over and over in the Torah, we see that the ancestors of the Jewish people, as great as they are, are human. And in *Noach*, we have an important reminder that even a "righteous" and "blameless" individual is still human.

After the flood, Noah and his family have the job of rebuilding the world. They build houses, have families, plant crops. They must have planted many different kinds of fruits and vegetables. The Torah doesn't give us a list, but it does tell us that Noah plants grapes and that from the grapes he makes wine. It also tells us that when the wine is ready, Noah drinks it, lots and lots of it, until he gets very drunk.

Does this sound like the behavior of a great person—to drink so much that he or she becomes very, very drunk? No, it doesn't. So why include this story in the book of Genesis? Maybe to remind us that this very righteous man is still human.

> *Can you think of one or two ways you could share you successes with friends without sounding like you're bragging?*

Think about it for a minute. Noah sees his world and all the people in it destroyed. He has the difficult job of keeping his family and the animals in the ark safe for a whole year while they all wait for the waters of the flood to dry up. He has to make sure the human race can restart and spread across the world. Do you think he felt pressured? Do you think that he might have had bad dreams, really bad dreams, about the world ending? If so, is it not possible that Noah drank so much wine in an effort to forget or to sleep without having such bad dreams? That's what many people would do, and in doing so, Noah reminds us that, after all, he is a person—a great one, but just a person.

> *When was the last time you tried something you weren't great at, like singing a song in front of friends or sharing a poem you wrote or trying to kick a soccer ball? What made you decide to try? How did you feel about being less than perfect at something?*

No One Likes a Showoff (Especially God)

There is a final lesson in *Noach* that has nothing to do with the flood but is there to again teach us about the importance of being the kind of person who tries to do good.

Do you know any showoffs? You know, the type of person who's always bragging about how good he or she is at sports or schoolwork or playing the guitar or computer games or just about anything? Their constant bragging can be more than annoying. It makes you think they believe they are somehow better than you, and maybe, just maybe, their bragging makes you feel less good about yourself.

We call this type of person "arrogant" or "egotistical," and the rabbis warn us about the dangers of being arrogant. In fact, they think that being arrogant is so bad that God says He can't live in the same world as arrogant people![3]

Unbelievable, isn't it? God doesn't want to be in the same world as people who brag and always tell you how great they are! God

---

3. Sotah 5a.

Noach (Gen 6:9–11:32)

doesn't say this about people who don't keep the Sabbath or don't keep kosher or don't keep any other commandment in the Torah. Only about arrogant people. And we have in *Noach* a story that gives us an example of how little patience God has for arrogant people.

The Torah tells us that after the flood, people move to a valley in the land of Shinar. Once there, they decide to build a city with a tower that touches the sky. They want to do this simply to show how great they are. Talk about being arrogant! As for God, He reacts just as you would expect. He is so unhappy that He stops their building and scatters them all over the world. Not only does God not want to live with them, He makes everyone speak different languages so that they can't all live with each other in the same place.

> *Do the tower builders get the message? Do they understand that their arrogance is a bad thing? It's not clear from the text. But careful readers of this story certainly do see the dangers of arrogance and why we should always try to avoid it.*

Lech Lecha

(Gen 12:1–17:27)

PART ONE—WHAT IT MEANS TO BE JEWISH

Up to now, the Torah has been telling us about our earliest ancestors, the first men and women. It shared with us exciting stories, like those of Adam and Eve, of Noah and the flood, and of the people who tried to build a tower that reached the heavens. In *Lech Lecha*, the Torah turns its attention to the story of the Jewish people. Before we can start that story, we need to talk a bit about what it means to be Jewish.

What do you think about when someone asks you what it means to be Jewish? Maybe it means following certain commandments, like keeping the Sabbath and eating only kosher food. That's a good answer, but it's not the only one, in part because there are many different ways people keep commandments. What we see in *Lech Lecha* is that being Jewish really comes down to serving God. And so, what we need to ask is . . .

How Do We Serve God?

Since the Torah tells us the story of Abraham and Sarah to help us understand what it means to be Jewish, we need to point out the obvious. The Jewish people got the Torah from God hundreds of years after Abraham and Sarah lived. This means that Abraham and Sarah served God (and we still don't know what this means) without having the Torah and its many commandments. So obviously, by telling us about the lives of the first Jews, who lived before there were commandments, the Torah is teaching us that serving God means more than just keeping the commandments.

Surprised? If you were, you won't be after we think about what serving God really means.

Here is one possible answer to this question. Later in the Torah, in the book of Deuteronomy, we read that we should "walk after God."[1] But this, too, is confusing. What exactly does it mean to "walk after God"? The rabbis of the Talmud who discuss the meaning of the Torah explain that walking with God means to walk after the characteristics of God.[2] And by "walk after," they mean imitate the characteristics of God.

In other words, to serve God means to be like God! And how can we be like God? The rabbis of the Talmud give us some important examples. For instance, Adam and Eve will have no home when God tells them leave the garden. Worse still, they will have no clothes, either! God gives them clothes before sending them away. And while we generally don't meet many naked people running around, there are people in our cities who need clothing. We can and should follow God's example. We can and should give clothes to homeless people who need them to stay safe and warm.

Here's another example. We will soon learn that Abraham follows the command of God to circumcise himself when he is 99 years old. That had to hurt a lot! God knows this, and He personally comes to visit Abraham after his circumcision. We learn from this how important it is to visit friends and family members when they are sick.

There are many other examples, but the point should be clear. Serving God means taking some of His characteristics and making them our own. Things like being kind and charitable and patient

---

1. Deut 13:5.
2. Sotah 14a.

and truthful. Not losing our temper. Not holding a grudge against someone else. When it comes to such things, God does not have to command us. He *shows* us how to act. We see this over and over in the stories in the book of Genesis, and by following God's example, we learn to become better people. That is what He wants from us, and that is what serving God is all about.

Of course, if serving God is about being like God, you might be asking, why do we need commandments? The answer is pretty simple. God wants us to become better people and to make His world a better place. He gave us commandments to help us do both. In other words, commandments help us to serve God and to become better people, and in this way, we are doing just what God wants from us.

Why Does God Give Us Tests?

When thinking about what it means to be Jewish, there is one other question we need to answer, because we see it throughout the story of Abraham and Sarah and in our own lives, too. And the question has to do with tests.

The rabbis of the Talmud tell us that God tests Abraham ten times to show how much He, God, loves Abraham.[3] But if we stop and think about it for a minute, doesn't this seem strange? Do parents "test" their children to show their love for them? Do friends do this to one another?

Maybe God tests Abraham to be sure that he, Abraham, really believes in Him. But this, too, is hard to understand. God, because He is God, knows that Abraham really believes in Him and really loves Him and really wants to serve Him. God needs no tests to know this. Is it possible, then, that it is Abraham himself who needs these tests?

Yes, it is very possible, and you probably can understand how this is so. Imagine that you have a project you are working on for school. As part of this project, you have to stand in front of the class and share what you've done (like students do for "show and tell").

---

3. Pirkei Avot 5:3.

You're a little nervous about it (or perhaps even very nervous). Your parents tell you you'll do fine. Your teacher tells you that you're very well prepared. They all tell you that there is no need to be nervous. But you are, because despite what everyone tells you, you're not completely sure you can stand in front of the class and share your work. Only after you've done so and done great do you relax. Now you know you can do it!

Now imagine Abraham. He is the first person in a long time—perhaps the first person since Adam and Eve—to really believe in God. Abraham tells himself that he believes in God and that he is ready to do whatever God asks of him. But until God asks, how does Abraham know for sure? And so, God, who understands Abraham's nervousness, tests him. Not once, but ten times. Each time Abraham passes one of these tests, he grows more sure of himself and of his belief in God. God never questions Abraham's belief. He just "tests" him so that Abraham won't question his own belief.

There is a second reason why these tests are so important, not just for Abraham but for all his children and grandchildren and great grandchildren, all the way up to our time. Abraham is the first Jew. He (along with Sarah) sets an example of how a person can believe in God and how a person who believes in God should act. We know that Abraham has no doubts about God, because he passes every test God gives him. We see that no matter how difficult things were or how hard each test is, Abraham always rises to the occasion. With each test, his faith in God remains as strong as ever.

This is an important reminder to us all. We hope and pray that things always go well for us. But if sometimes life gets difficult, for us or for our families or for our friends, we can look to the example of Abraham and know that just like him, we, too, can pass the tests that God may give us. We, too, can grow stronger with each "test" we pass.

Lech Lecha

(Gen 12:1–17:27)

PART TWO—THE STORY OF ABRAHAM AND SARAH BEGINS

Summary of This Week's Reading

Lech Lecha begins with a test for Abraham, who is still called by the name Abram. (God will change his and his wife's names later in the story, so be patient. It will all be explained.) God tells Abram to leave his homeland and his family and go "to the land which I will show you." Abram and his wife Sarai (whose name will later be changed to Sarah) head for this unknown land, taking their nephew Lot with them. When they arrive at this place, called Canaan, Abram builds an altar to pray to God. Then, as the midrash tells us, he and Sarai begin to teach the people they meet about the one, true God.

    Abram and Sarai had not been in Canaan very long before they realized there was no food anywhere. There was not enough rain for the crops to grow, so there was a terrible famine in the land. Abram and Sarai are forced to go down to Egypt to try and find food. But Egypt is a dangerous place, especially for women as beautiful as Sarai. Abram and Sarai try to protect themselves by saying they are brother and sister instead of husband and wife. This doesn't work so well, and Sarai is kidnapped and taken to the king's palace. (The king of Egypt in those days was called "Pharaoh.") God saves Sarai by forcing Pharaoh to return her to Abram. Pharaoh also gives them gold, silver, and cattle to try and make up for what he did.

When they return to Canaan, Lot, who was with Abram and Sarai in Egypt, decides he'd rather live by himself. He moves to the city of Sodom (a really bad place that we'll learn more about in the next week's Torah reading). A war breaks out, and Lot is taken prisoner by one of the armies. When Abram hears this, he quickly goes and rescues his nephew.

At this point in the story, Abram is a little sad. It's true that he saved his nephew, but he has no children of his own. God appears to Abram in a deep, dark dream. He tells Abram that he will someday have a child, and He promises Abram that his descendants (that is, his children, grandchildren, great grandchildren, and so on) will be "as numerous as the stars of the heavens." But before this happens, Abram's descendants will leave the land of Canaan and be made slaves for four hundred years.

Abram awakes, both happy about someday having a child and a little scared about his descendants being slaves. Ten years pass, and he and Sarai still have no children. In those days, men could have more than one wife, so Sarai tells Abram to marry her servant Hagar. Maybe, Sarai thinks, Hagar will have a child with Abram, and since Hagar is her servant, it will be a little like having a child of her own.

This sounds like a good plan, but when Hagar gets pregnant, she starts to brag about how she was able to have a child and Sarai wasn't, and Sarai becomes a little jealous. Sarai, who is still Hagar's boss, treats her in a mean way, so Hagar runs away. An angel appears to Hagar and convinces her to return by telling her that the son she will have, Ishmael, will be the father of a great nation. Abram is 86 years old when Ishmael is born.

Fast forward 13 years. God decides it's time for name changes. Abram becomes Abraham. Sarai becomes Sarah. The name change, you see, is symbolic. Maybe Abram and Sarai can't have children, but Abraham and Sarah certainly will. This is what God tells Abraham, and God adds that Abraham should call the child he and Sarah will have Isaac.

LECH LECHA (GEN 12:1-17:27)

There is one more thing that must happen before Abraham can have children. He must circumcise himself. God tells him that the circumcision is a sign of the special connection between God and what will become the Jewish people. Abraham does this immediately (he is 99 years old at the time), and he has all the men of his household (including Ishmael, who is 13 years old) circumcised, too.

Life Lessons from Lech Lecha

We saw from the summary of this week's reading that a lot is going on in the lives of Abraham and Sarah. They move to a new country. They go down to Egypt to escape a famine. Lot leaves. Abraham takes Hagar as a wife. Ishmael is born. Most important, God makes a covenant (called *brit* in Hebrew) with Abraham. A covenant is like a really strong promise, and in our story, God promises the land of Israel to Abraham and all his family who will come after him. Abraham, in return, promises to always believe in God.

As you should expect by now, these happenings and these stories have many important lessons for us. Let's look at three in particular.

Serving God with Joy

We began this chapter of *Lech Lecha* by thinking about how we can best serve God. We saw that this means trying to be like God by being kind and merciful and honest. By caring for others. By trying to become better people, and in doing so, making the world a better place.

Abraham and Sarah understand this and do these things throughout their lives. But in *Lech Lecha*, they show us another important way to serve God: with joy.

Stop and think about it for a minute. Abraham and Sarah face many difficult challenges in these chapters. God tells them to leave their homeland and families and head to an unknown land. They get to this land, Canaan, and soon have to leave because of the famine. They have problems with Pharaoh in Egypt. Abraham has to go to war to save Lot. These are not easy things, and yet, do Abraham and Sarah complain? Not at all. Just the opposite! When Abraham arrives in Canaan, he builds an altar to pray to God and to thank Him. In fact, all through the book of Genesis, we have stories of Abraham building altars to pray to and thank God.

Abraham understands that God is part of his life, always. Abraham sees that God has a plan for him, even if he doesn't know, or perhaps doesn't even understand, all the details of God's plan. But Abraham (and Sarah, too) are sure of one thing: God only wants the best for them.

If each of us can remember this, that God only wants the best for us, we will see just how easy it can be to serve God with joy.

> *Do you have certain jobs to do around your house, like making your bed each morning or taking out the garbage? Do your parents have to remind you to do them? Do you ever complain when you do these jobs? How does that make your parents feel? How does it make you feel?*

Things Don't Always Go According to Plan

There is an old saying in Yiddish: *Mann tracht, un Gott lacht.* If your grandparents or great-grandparents know Yiddish, they can tell you what this means. For those of us who don't speak Yiddish or don't have Yiddish-speaking grandparents, here is what it means in English: "Man plans, and God laughs."

Despite what you might think, this saying does not mean that God is making fun of us or laughing at the things we do. What it is trying to tell us is that even our most carefully made plans don't always work out the way we think they will. And *Lech Lecha* has a very good example of how plans can go wrong.

Abraham and Sarah were married a long, long time without having any children. Like many people, they want children. They especially want children who can help with their mission of teaching the people of Canaan about the one, true God. They are patient. They are hopeful, until one day they aren't. It is at this point that Sarah has what she thinks is a great idea. In those days, a man could

Lech Lecha (Gen 12:1–17:27)

have more than one wife. Sarah tells Abraham to take Hagar, her servant, as a wife. Because Hagar is a servant, any child she has would be thought of as also being Sarah's child. Sarah and Abraham could then raise this child and teach him or her how to teach others about God.

Sounds great, right? So what went wrong? Hagar is a servant, and sometimes servants aren't treated with the respect all people deserve. And even if they are respected, servants know who the really important people in the house are (the masters) and who the less important people are (them). But unexpectedly, Hagar the servant becomes Abraham's other wife. She now feels important. She is now treated as an important person. And once she becomes pregnant, she begins to think she is even more important than Sarah. She begins to act like she's more important than Sarah and to talk to Sarah like she is the most important woman in Abraham's life (which she isn't!).

This is not what Sarah expected. This is not how she thought her plan would work out. What should she do now? What can she do?

It is true that Hagar does not act in a nice way toward Sarah once she becomes Abraham's wife. She even makes fun of Sarah because she doesn't have any children of her own. Despite this, Sarah could have tried to understand better what Hagar was feeling. Maybe after being a servant for so many years, Hagar thinks it's *her* turn to act all important.

It would have been hard for her to do, but Sarah could have also tried to explain to Hagar how her words and actions were hurtful. She doesn't. Instead, she gets upset and angry and then demands that Abraham send Hagar away. Abraham is confused by all this and asks God what he should do. God tells Abraham to do whatever Sarah says, and so, with a broken heart, he sends Hagar and the baby, Ishmael, away. Only because God sends an angel to speak to Hagar does she return to Abraham. But the bad feelings remain between her and Sarah.

This is not a good solution for any of them.

There are many reasons why the Torah tells us this story of Hagar and Sarah. We see that although Abraham loves Ishmael very much, it will be Isaac who continues the work of his parents to teach the world about God. We see how great Sarah is, because God tells Abraham to listen to her and to do what she says. But we also see what happens when people get angry and jealous.

Sarah has a plan. It doesn't work out. This sometimes happens to all of us, and when it does, we need to remember that things happen and that getting upset won't change them. Just look at this story. Sarah is a great person. A very special person. But even the most special people can make bad decisions when they get angry or upset or jealous. Sarah does. It would have been better for her to have thought about what to do with Hagar without anger and without jealousy. Had she done so, maybe she would have found a better solution to her problem.

> *Can you think of a time when you made a good decision when you were angry or upset? If not, what does that tell you? What do you think you can do to stop making decisions when you are angry and upset?*

The Importance of Family

Lech Lecha begins with God telling Abraham to leave his homeland and family and go to an unknown land. This is a difficult test for Abraham, because family is very important to him. We see this in his relationship with his wife, Sarah, with both his sons, Isaac and Ishmael, and with his nephew Lot.

When Lot is just a boy, his father, Haran, dies, and his uncle Abraham brings him to live in his home. Abraham treats Lot like a son. In fact, during the many years when Abraham and Sarah have no children of their own, they think that Lot will be their heir. In other words, they think that Lot will get all their flocks and possessions after they die and that he will continue the important work they are doing teaching people about God. So imagine their surprise when they return to Canaan from Egypt and Lot tells them that he is moving far away from them!

We are never told exactly why Lot decides to leave. Some think he found it difficult to live with people as great as Abraham and Sarah. Lot is a good person, but he is no Abraham. Others think Lot

Lech Lecha (Gen 12:1–17:27)

wants to make his own fortune and not depend on Abraham and Sarah for money and flocks. No matter why he leaves, we can be sure that his leaving makes Abraham and Sarah very sad.

What happens next teaches us just how important family should be.

When Lot leaves Abraham and Sarah, he moves to the city of Sodom. Shortly after he arrives, Sodom is caught in the middle of a war between two mighty armies, and Lot is taken prisoner by the stronger of these two armies. Abraham hears what happens to his nephew and immediately leaves on a rescue mission. He takes a small number of men with him, 318 in all, and is able to defeat this mighty army and rescue Lot.

Stop for a minute and think about this. Lot leaves him. Lot hurts him. The army that captures Lot is very large and very powerful. None of this stops Abraham. Lot is his nephew. Lot is like a son to him, and Abraham understands that family is among the most important things we have in life (maybe the most important).

This might be a good thing to think about the next time your brother or sister annoys you!

What one thing you think is special about your family?
What is one thing you really enjoy doing with your family?
How do these help you appreciate your family?

Vayera

(Gen 18:1–22:24)

VISITORS AND MORE VISITORS

Summary of This Week's Reading

Vayera begins three days after Abraham has circumcised himself. God, and not an angel, comes to visit Abraham. Not with a message or a vision. Just to visit him. But Abraham, who is always looking for opportunities to host guests and be hospitable, sees three men (at least, he thinks they're men) approaching his tent. Abraham rushes off to prepare a meal for them. These guests are really angels disguised as men, and one of them tells Abraham that in exactly one year, his wife Sarah will give birth to a son.

As was the custom in those days, the men and women eat separately. But Sarah is close enough to hear the news about her having a child. She laughs, thinking that it's impossible, because she's so old (almost 90). God is not happy with her laughter or her doubts.

The angels leave and head toward Sodom. They have a mission to destroy the town because the people who live there are so evil. Even so, God decides that He should tell Abraham of His plans, because Abraham and his descendants will "keep the way of the Lord to perform righteousness and justice." When Abraham hears this news, he tries to convince God not to destroy Sodom. "Maybe there are 50 righteous people there," argues Abraham. "It would be wrong to destroy righteous people because of their evil neighbors." God agrees, and so the debate begins. Abraham keeps asking, "What if there are fewer righteous people than You thought? What if there are 40 or 30 or even 20?" God listens to Abraham's arguments, until he reaches ten. At that point, God ends the discussion, but He has heard Abraham. He will save the righteous people of Sodom.

To do this, two of the three disguised angels arrive in the doomed city. Abraham's nephew Lot lives there, and just as he learned from his uncle, he extends his hospitality to them. He even protects them from the people of Sodom, who hate strangers and want to hurt them. The two guests then tell Lot that they have come to destroy Sodom but will save him and his family, because they are the only righteous people there. Sadly, two of his daughters do not believe the warning, and they stay in Sodom. Lot, his wife, and his other two daughters run away as fast as they can. The angels tell them not to look back and watch the city being destroyed, but Lot's wife is very curious. She does look back and is turned into a pillar of salt as punishment.

The story returns to Abraham, who moves to Gerar after Sodom is destroyed. Gerar is a little like Egypt, and Abraham and Sarah are afraid that she might be kidnapped. So, again, they tell people that they are brother and sister. The king of Gerar, Abimelech, doesn't care and takes Sarah to his palace. In a dream, God warns Abimelech that he will die unless he returns Sarah to her husband, Abraham. Abimelech does this, but he is angry. He asks Abraham why he pretended that he and Sarah were brother and sister. Abraham explains that he feared he would be killed by men who wanted the beautiful Sarah for themselves.

Once Abraham and Sarah leave Gerar, God remembers His promise to Sarah that she will have a son. She does have a son, and she names him Isaac, which means "he will laugh." She picks this name because she thinks everyone will laugh when they hear that an old lady like her had a baby. (Abraham is 100 years old and Sarah is 90 when Isaac is born.) Isaac is circumcised at the age of eight days.

But there are still more stories in this week's reading.

Vayera (Gen 18:1–22:24)

Sarah is still jealous of Hagar and is worried that Hagar's son, Ishmael, is a bad influence on Isaac. She tells Abraham to send them away. He does, but only after God tells him to listen to Sarah. Hagar and Ishmael wander in the desert until they run out of water to drink. Hagar believes Ishmael is about to die of thirst and prays to God to save him. God hears their suffering and saves Ishmael by showing his mother a well.

At this point, Vayera interrupts its stories to tell us that Abimelech makes a treaty with Abraham at Beersheba, where Abraham gives him seven sheep as a sign of their truce.

God has one last test for Abraham. (Remember our discussion about tests in the last chapter?) God tells Abraham to offer Isaac as a sacrifice on Mount Moriah (which is the place where the Temple will be built many years in the future). Abraham ties up Isaac (who lets himself be tied up, something we'll talk more about) and places him on the altar. Abraham is ready to actually sacrifice Isaac, but at the last second, an angel calls out and tells Abraham to stop. The angel tells Abraham that he passed the test and that God knows how strongly Abraham believes in Him. Just then, Abraham sees a ram caught in some bushes by its horns and sacrifices the ram in place of Isaac. (This is why the Jewish people blow a ram's horn, called a shofar, on Rosh Hashanah, the New Year, to remember this story.)

Vayera ends with Abraham receiving news of the birth of a daughter, Rebekah, to his nephew Bethuel. (We will learn more about Rebekah in the next two weekly readings.)

Life Lessons from Vayera

It's amazing to think about how many important stories are packed into each weekly reading, and this week is no exception. In fact, *Vayera* has in it one of the most important stories from the lives of Abraham and Sarah, and it is a story we remember each and every year.

Curious about this story? Good. Let's get started.

A Curious Student's Guide to the Book of Genesis

Walking in the Ways of God

We have already seen in our discussion of *Lech Lecha* that there is more than one way to serve God. Following the commandments is the one we most often think of, but acting like God—by being kind, patient, generous, and honest—is another way to do this. We call trying to be like God "walking in His ways," and this week's reading gives us an important example of how to do this.

If you remember, the previous weekly reading ended with Abraham circumcising himself and all the men in his household. Before we continue with the story, let's try an experiment. Ask the boys in your class whether they remember their circumcisions. Do any of them remember it? Of course not, because they were circumcised when they were eight days old. That is what God tells Abraham to do with his son. But Abraham is commanded by God to do this when he is 99 years old, and circumcision as an adult hurts. A lot.

This is when *Vayera* begins, three days after Abraham circumcises himself. The rabbis tell us that the third day after a circumcision is especially painful for an adult. It is easy to imagine that Abraham is not feeling very well. What does God do? He pays Abraham a visit. Not to give him a command (like He did when He told Abraham to leave his homeland). Not to show him a vision (like He did when Abraham dreamed about his descendants going down to a strange land and becoming slaves). Instead, God just comes to visit.

Sometimes we think that when we visit a sick friend, we have to bring a gift or do something special. Those are good things to do, but we learn from God's visit to Abraham that it is important just to visit the sick and that you can make a sick friend or family member feel better just by being there. Being there for another person when he or she doesn't feel well (or maybe when he or she just feels a little lonely) is what friends do. And it's what we do when we want to "walk in the ways of God."

> *Can you remember a time when you went to visit a friend or a family member who was sick? How did your visit make them feel? How did it make you feel? Who do you think got more out of the visit, you or your friend?*

Vayera (Gen 18:1–22:24)

Honoring God by Serving People

Did you ever stop to think why Moses came down from Mount Sinai with *two* stone tablets? Did God have so much to share with Moses that it couldn't fit on one tablet? Of course not! God can do anything, and if He had wanted to give Moses only one tablet, He would have. So why two?

Here's why. There are two tablets to teach us that there are two kinds of commandments.

What God writes on the first tablet involves how we interact with Him—things like praying to Him and keeping the Sabbath. God also gives us other laws in the Torah, like having a Passover seder, blowing a shofar on Rosh Hashanah, and building a sukkah on Sukkot. These kinds of commandments have a special name: commandments between humans and God.

What God writes on the second tablet involves how we interact with other people—things like not stealing from others or lying to them. God also gives us other laws in the Torah about interacting with other people, like caring for the sick, giving charity, and being hospitable to guests. And guess what? These kinds of commandments have a special name, too: commandments between humans and other humans.

If you were to guess which of these was more important, those between humans and God or between humans and other humans, what would you say? Many people would say that commandments involving God are always more important, because, well, they involve God. *Vayera* and God's visit to Abraham teach us something different.

Let's get back to the story.

God has come to be with Abraham, and that must make Abraham feel special. However, in the middle of this visit, Abraham sees three men approaching his tent. Abraham is famous for his hospitality. He is always looking to host guests. In fact, his tent is open on all four sides so that he can see people approaching from any direction.

What to do? God is there, visiting him. How dare he leave God's presence to greet these three men and offer them a meal? But that is exactly what he does! Abraham begs God, saying: "Please my Lord, if I have found favor in your eyes, do not leave!" Abraham rushes off to welcome the men (who are really angels there to tell him that Sarah will have a baby in one year, but Abraham doesn't know that). What does God do? He waits, and by waiting, He shows us that the commandments between humans and other humans can even be more important than those between humans and God.

You would never say such a thing. The rabbis would never say such a thing. Only God can, because people acting kindly toward one another brings peace to the world. People acting kindly toward one another are also serving God by walking in His ways. So, really, when we follow the commandments between humans and other humans, we are at the same time following the commandments between humans and God.

> *Your family probably has guests over a lot. How do you help your parents when they entertain guests? Would you stop playing with your friends to help your parents with this?*

Always Do Right

All of us, adults and young people, spend our lives trying to do what's right and trying not to do what's wrong. When we know the difference—and it's usually pretty easy to tell the difference—we know what to do. But what happens when we see someone who is older than we are or smarter than we are about to do something we think is wrong? Should we stop them? May we stop them?

This is the challenge Abraham faces in *Vayera*.

In the days of Abraham, there are two important and powerful cities, Sodom and Gomorrah, and the people who live there are evil. The Torah does not tell us exactly what their sins are, but their sins are so great and so many that God decides to destroy the cities. But before He does so, He decides to tell Abraham what He is about to do. Why, you might ask? That's a good question, and the Torah gives us a good answer. God knows that Abraham will teach his children and his grandchildren to do "what is just and right," so

Vayera (Gen 18:1–22:24)

God appears to Abraham to tell him that destroying these two cities is "just and right."

There is only one problem. Abraham does not think this is a "just and right" thing to do. Maybe, he thinks, not every single person in these cities is wicked. Maybe by destroying both cities, God would destroy the innocent along with the guilty! But Abraham thinks of himself as nothing but "dust and ashes" compared to God. How dare he, Abraham, challenge God?

Abraham dares. He argues with God and tries to convince Him not to destroy Sodom and Gomorrah. "Maybe there are 50 righteous people there," says Abraham. "It would be wrong to destroy righteous people because of their evil neighbors." God agrees, and so the debate begins. Abraham asks, "What if there are 45 righteous people? Or 40? Or 30? Or 20? Or even only 10?" At this point, God ends the discussion, but He has heard Abraham. He will save the righteous people (who happen to be Abraham's nephew Lot and his family).

What an important life lesson this is! God had to know that Abraham would argue with Him. After all, God Himself says that Abraham will teach his children and his grandchildren to do "what is just and right." Perhaps God tells Abraham of His plan to destroy the two cities just to give Abraham a chance to argue with Him, to try and convince God to do "what is just and right." By giving Abraham the opportunity to argue with Him, and by letting the debate go on and on, God is showing us the importance of always standing up for what is right and of always doing what is right, even if it means arguing with God Himself!

> *How would you act if you thought one of your teachers or your parents was doing something wrong? How might you try to convince them that there was a better way? By talking with them? By showing them? Would you do this before they did the thing that seemed wrong or would you only talk to them after they did it?*

A Curious Student's Guide to the Book of Genesis

A Very Famous but Very Difficult Story

At the beginning of this chapter, we said that *Vayera* has a very famous story in it that we remember every year. That story is about Abraham offering his son Isaac as a sacrifice to God. This is a very difficult story to understand, even for adults and even for our greatest scholars and teachers. So we aren't going to try to find life lessons from it to share with you. But there are a few details in the story you should know.

First, God does not tell Abraham to sacrifice Isaac. He tells him to *offer* Isaac as a sacrifice. What's the difference? This is a big test for Abraham. In fact, it is his tenth and final test. Had God told him to sacrifice Isaac, passing the test would have meant killing Isaac. God certainly doesn't want that! But by *offering* Isaac, which means tying him up and putting him on the altar, Abraham does exactly what God asks, and so he passes the test.

What a minute, you must be saying! Why would God even ask such a thing? To answer this, we need a short history lesson. In Abraham's time, many nations worshipped their idols by offering human sacrifices. God wants to stop this practice, and so He tells Abraham to offer Isaac as a sacrifice. At the very last minute, just when it appears that Abraham will go through with it, God tells him to stop. In this way, God makes it very clear to everyone that He has no interest in human sacrifice.

In the end, Abraham does offer a sacrifice to God. He sacrifices a ram that he finds tangled up in the bushes, and that is why the Jewish people sound a ram's horn (a shofar) every year on Rosh Hashanah: to remember this story.

Second, we always seem to talk about this story as a test of Abraham. It is, but it is a test of Isaac, too. How so? Isaac is 37 years old, which is much younger (100 years younger!) than Abraham. He is stronger and faster. He could have easily run away once he realized what Abraham intended to do. But he doesn't. He lets his father tie him up and place him on the altar. Isaac has no way of knowing that God will stop Abraham at the last minute. Isaac only knows that God has commanded that he, Isaac, be offered as a sacrifice, and Isaac, like his father Abraham, is prepared to do whatever God asks

VAYERA (GEN 18:1–22:24)

of him. That's what all of Abraham's tests are about: being willing to do what God asks.

There is a lot to think about and to say about this story. But if you remember these two facts—that God tells Abraham to offer Isaac as a sacrifice and that this is also a test for Isaac—you will be better able to retell the story as it's presented in this week's reading.

Chayei Sarah

(Gen 23:1–25:18)

CHANGES IN THE FAMILY

Summary of This Week's Reading

In Chayei Sarah, the main characters change, because Sarah dies, at the age of 127. Abraham, of course, is very sad, and he buys a special place to bury Sarah, a cave in the Machpelah field, which is near the town of Hebron. Abraham buys the cave from Ephron the Hittite for 400 silver coins, and while you cannot go into the cave itself, you can still visit it today if you travel to Israel. (The town is still called Hebron, just as it is in the Torah!)

After burying Sarah, Abraham understands that big changes must be made in his life. So he tells his servant Eliezer to go to Haran (the place where Abraham was born) to look for a wife for Isaac. (Somehow, Abraham knows that the local Canaanite women would not be a good match for Isaac.)

Eliezer leaves on this important mission, but he is worried. How will he know who is the right woman to become Isaac's wife?

Like Abraham, Eliezer believes in the one, true God, so he prays and asks God to give him a sign. What kind of sign? Eliezer tells God that when he arrives in Haran, he will ask the young women there for a drink of water. If one of the women says, "Certainly, and I'll also give your camels some water, too," he will know that she is the one to marry Isaac. It seems that God hears Eliezer's prayer, because as soon as he arrives, a girl hears him ask for some water. She quickly offers to give him and his camels water to drink. (This is a big deal, because Eliezer has ten camels, and as you know, camels drink a lot of water.)

As she brings Eliezer water, they begin to talk, and he learns that the girl, Rebekah, is the daughter of Abraham's nephew, Bethuel. Rebekah then runs home to tell her family about the man at the well. Her brother Laban greets the servant and invites him to spend the night. Eliezer goes on to tell Rebekah's family why he has come to Haran, and he even tells them about his prayer to God and the sign that Rebekah was meant to be the wife of his master's son. Rebekah's family agrees to the proposed match, and that very night, they make a big party to celebrate.

In the morning, Eliezer tells the family that he very much wants to go back to Abraham, to share the good news and to introduce Rebekah to Isaac. However, before he can leave, he and Rebekah's family ask her again if she agrees to all this. (Even though she is a young girl, Eliezer understands that she has the right to decide on her own whom to marry.) Rebekah says yes, and she and Eliezer set off for Canaan. There, she meets and marries Isaac, who has been very sad since his mother died three years ago. Once he marries Rebekah, he is able to feel happy again.

But Isaac is not the only person to get married in this week's reading. Abraham gets married again, to a woman named Ketura (who may or may not have been Hagar, but that is a long, complicated story). He has six more sons with Ketura. Before his death, however, Abraham gives gifts to his other children and sends them all away, because he knows that it is Isaac who will carry on the important work of teaching people about the one, true God.

Chayei Sarah ends with the death of Abraham at the age of 175. Isaac, with the help of his half-brother Ishmael, buries their father in the cave of Machpelah, next to his beloved wife Sarah. Since Ishmael returns home to help bury his father, this reading briefly lists the names of his children. This list serves as a kind of introduction to the next week's reading, Toldot, which begins the story of Isaac and his sons.

CHAYEI SARAH (GEN 23:1–25:18)

Life Lessons from Chayei Sarah

Chayei Sarah has a single theme: change. It explains how the leadership of one family, which will eventually become the Jewish people, changes. Sarah and Abraham die, and Isaac and Rebekah become the focus of the story of the beginnings of the Jewish people. And because it is about change, *Chayei Sarah* doesn't have a lot of stories—only two, actually: how Abraham buys a place to bury Sarah and how Eliezer goes on and completes his mission to find a wife for Isaac. All the same, it does have some important lessons for us.

Let's take a good look at those lessons.

The Importance of Women

Think about your favorite story books. Do they take place in another country? Do they take place in a different time (the past or the future)? One of the things that make stories about different places and times so interesting is that they are different. And not just in the ways the characters dress or even talk. People from different places and different times than ours have different customs. They do things differently. They act differently.

Sometimes these differences seem strange to us. Sometimes they seem wrong or unfair. For example, when we read stories from our past, we sometimes see that people of color are treated differently, that they do not have the same rights and freedoms they have in America today. (If you doubt this, ask anyone who was alive in the 1950s or 1960s about separate water fountains and whites-only restaurants and movie theaters.)

The same is true for women. If this is hard to understand, just remember that women couldn't vote in America until 1920, even though America became an independent country in 1776!

Maybe you're wondering, what does all this have to do with *Chayei Sarah* or even with the book of Genesis? A lot, actually, because the stories we read in Genesis tell us of a different time, when men were mostly in charge of—well, everything, and women were expected to stay at home and be good, obedient daughters and then wives. These stories take place in a time when sons inherited everything, and daughters—well, sometimes they were hidden in boxes.[1]

When we read these stories and compare them to how people act and are treated in our time, it is easy to think that the women in Genesis—women like Sarah and Rebekah—aren't very important. This week's reading comes to tell us that this is just not true.

Let's start with the name of this week's reading: *Chayei Sarah*. This name means "the years of Sarah's life." Why would we have a Torah portion about the years of Sarah's life if she was so unimportant?

Rabbi Shlomo Riskin, the Chief Rabbi of Efrat, sees in the name of this week's reading proof of how important Sarah is and what a great influence she has on all who know her. Rabbi Riskin thinks that we have a weekly reading about the years of Sarah's life because she, not Abraham, is really the more important person during the time they both live.

What a minute, you must be saying. What about all the stories of Abraham? His ten tests? His being told to offer his son as a sacrifice? Even when the angels come to tell Abraham and Sarah that Sarah will give birth to a son, they talk to Abraham, while Sarah is sitting back in the tent!

Yes, that is all true, but that is also how life was in those days. Visitors would meet with the man, not with his wife. He served the meal while she stood hidden away, busying herself with the cooking. But—and here is the point Rabbi Riskin is making about the name of this week's reading—Abraham lives 38 more years after Sarah dies. What does he accomplish after Sarah dies? He sends his servant to find a wife for Isaac. He takes a new/old wife and has six more sons, but we know nothing about them or about his time with them.

In other words, once Sarah dies, it is as if Abraham becomes less important. It seems that he is in our story only until Isaac marries Rebekah, and then the two of them become our main focus.

---

1. The midrash states that Jacob hides his daughter Dinah in a box when the family first meets Esau upon their return to Canaan after living with Laban for 20 years.

Chayei Sarah (Gen 23:1–25:18)

That is why this week's reading is called "the years of Sarah's life": because Sarah gives these years importance.

Still not convinced?

Remember when Sarah was so concerned about the bad influence Ishmael had on Isaac when Isaac was a small boy? She told Abraham to send Ishmael and Hagar away. This bothered Abraham a lot, because he truly loved his son Ishmael. He didn't know what to do. So he turned to God for advice, and what did God tell him? Listen to your wife. She knows better. Send Ishmael away. From this, the midrash learns that "Abraham was second to Sarah in prophetic power."

From our perspective, it might seem like the women of Genesis are secondary to their husbands. They are not. We have seen time and again how important Sarah is to Abraham and to the Jewish people they are working to create. We will see it again in next week's reading of *Toldot* (Gen 25:19–28:9) when Rebekah decides to take matters into her own hands when it comes to the blessing Jacob will receive.

Chayei Sarah is here in part to remind us that the Jews exist as a people not only because of the patriarchs, Abraham, Isaac, and Jacob, but also because of the matriarchs, Sarah, Rebekah, Rachel, and Leah.

> *Ask your grandparents about certain jobs people had when they were little. Were there "men's jobs" and "women's jobs"? Talk with them about what made a job right for men or right for women. Then try to figure out if that is still true today.*

Knowing What's Important in Another Person

Have you ever had a new student join your class? Do you remember what you thought when you first met him or her? Did you notice his clothes? Her shoes? What color her hair was? Was his hair straight or curly? Did he talk with an accent? Was her skin darker or lighter than yours?

If you did, you were simply doing what most of us do. When we meet new people, we tend to look at them and try to see what we can figure out about them by their appearance. This is called a "first impression." You might guess something right about new people by the way they look, but you can't really get to know them this way.

How do you really get to know a person? A good start is talking to them. Or watching the things they do and how they speak with other people and how they treat other people.

This is what Eliezer does when he goes to find a wife for Isaac. When he prays to God to help him in his mission, Eliezer does not ask to find a beautiful woman or a rich woman. He instead asks for one who will offer him water to drink and then offer to water his camels. In other words, he is looking for someone who is kind and generous and helpful. And once Rebekah volunteers to do this, Eliezer watches her.

What does he see? He sees a young woman who quickly gives him and his camels some water and who runs back to the well again and again to get more. When Eliezer sees how eager she is to do this good deed and how she literally runs to finish it, he remembers how his master Abraham acted when the three angels came to visit him. Abraham was eager to offer them food and drink, and he ran to prepare their meal. He asked Sarah to quickly bake bread. He even told Ishmael to run and get calves to slaughter and serve as part of the meal.

What Eliezer sees in Rebekah are the same *middot*, the same character traits, that Abraham and Sarah possess and that they teach their son Isaac. A woman with these same character traits will of course be a good match for Isaac.

This is the real lesson of Eliezer's prayer to God. Eliezer knows that he can look at a woman and know whether she is beautiful. But that's not what he is looking for. He needs help knowing the real person, because he doesn't have weeks or even days to talk to women and watch their actions. His master wants him to return quickly. Eliezer understands that to complete his mission quickly, he needs God's help. With God's help, something as simple as asking for a little water to drink can teach Eliezer all he needs to know about the true character of the young woman.

Chayei Sarah (Gen 23:1–25:18)

Next time you meet a new person, try to remember the lesson that Eliezer's story teaches us. It's okay to notice what a person looks like or how he or she dresses. But getting to really know a person takes time, and that is how we make true friends.

Try to remember the first time you met your best friend. Can you remember what you first thought about him or her? And now that you know this person and are friends with him or her, do you think your first impression was correct? Or did your first impression make it harder for the two of you to become friends?

Toldot

(Gen 25:19–28:9)

WHEN MOM AND DAD CAN'T AGREE

Summary of This Week's Reading

Toldot begins by reminding us that Isaac is the son of Abraham and that Abraham is Isaac's father. How strange. We have read so many stories about them that we know this already! But the rabbis learn an interesting fact from this. They say that Isaac looked exactly like his father—so much so that even when he was a little boy, people would see Isaac and say, "You must be Abraham's son!" (We will talk more about this shortly.)

After introducing us again to Isaac, Toldot tells us that Isaac and Rebekah want to start a family but aren't able to have children for 20 years. They both pray to God, and their prayers are finally answered. Rebekah becomes pregnant with twins. But things don't go well for her. The babies in her belly fight all the time. She is confused and frightened by this, and so she asks God what's going on. He tells her that "there are two nations in your womb" and that the younger will rule over the elder. This is exciting news, but for some reason, she doesn't share it with Isaac. (We will also talk more about this.)

When the babies are born, Esau comes first, and he is large and hairy. Then comes his brother, Jacob, who is born holding onto Esau's heel. As they grow up, Esau becomes a hunter and a person who loves the outdoors. (The Torah calls him "a man of the field.") Jacob is very different. He is quiet and likes to be on his own—so much so that the Torah calls him a person who "lives in tents." Toldot adds one other very important fact: Isaac favors Esau, and Rebekah loves Jacob.

When the boys are teenagers, Esau comes back from the fields one day very tired and very hungry. He finds Jacob cooking a pot of red lentil soup. He tells Jacob that he is starving and asks him for some of the soup. Esau is so very, very hungry that he trades his birthright (the special things he should get because he's the firstborn) to Jacob for some of that soup. (Because of this, the Torah gives Esau a nickname, Edom, which comes from the Hebrew word for red, just like the soup.)

Toldot now switches back to the story of Isaac and Rebekah. Just like in the time of Abraham, there is a famine, and they have no food to eat. So, Isaac and Rebekah travel down to Gerar, just like Abraham and Sarah did. When they get there, Isaac tells people that Rebekah is his sister, just like Abraham told people that Sarah was his sister. And just like Abraham and Sarah, Isaac and Rebekah have to leave Gerar when people discover that they are really husband and wife. (Isaac copying his father is something else that we will soon talk about.)

When he returns from Gerar, Isaac begins to farm the land. God blesses him so that his fields grow 100 times more crops than any of the other fields around them. In this way, Isaac becomes very wealthy. He also notices that the Philistines have filled in all the wells that his father Abraham dug. (Israel doesn't get much rain, so wells were very important.) Isaac reopens the wells dug by Abraham and even calls them by the same names that Abraham used. Isaac then digs three new wells. The Philistines argue with him about the first two, but there are no arguments about the third new well that Isaac digs.

We then learn that Esau marries two Hittite women, which makes his parents very sad.

By this time, Isaac is old and blind. He is worried that he may die soon, and he wants to bless his favored son Esau before he dies. Isaac asks Esau to make him a delicious meal before he blesses him. Rebekah hears all this and is very upset. She thinks that Jacob should get this special blessing from Isaac. While Esau goes off to hunt for food, Rebekah dresses Jacob in Esau's clothes and covers his arms and neck with goatskin to make him feel like his hairier brother. She also cooks some of Isaac's favorite food, and she sends Jacob to give this food to his father.

Now the story gets complicated. Isaac isn't sure which son is giving him the food. Could Esau have come back from hunting so quickly? Isaac asks, "Who are you?" Jacob answers, "It is I." He is not really lying, but he is not being completely honest either. He is being very tricky, which is what his mother told him to do.

In the end, Jacob receives his father's special blessing, which includes ruling over his brother. Jacob leaves through the back of Isaac's tent just as Esau comes in through the front. Isaac now knows he has been tricked, but he says, "Let him keep the blessing I gave him." This makes Esau very sad. He cries and begs his father for a blessing. All Isaac can do now is to predict two things: that Esau will live by his sword and that if Jacob messes up somehow, he will no longer rule over his older brother, Esau.

As you can imagine, Esau is very, very angry, so angry that he wants to kill Jacob. Rebekah tells Jacob to run away from Esau and to go to Haran, where her brother Laban lives. She also wants him to find a wife from Laban's family.

Toldot concludes with Esau hearing that Jacob has gone to Haran to find a wife who comes from their family. He therefore decides to take a third wife: Machalath, the daughter of his uncle Ishmael.

Life Lessons from Toldot

The stories in *Toldot* are complicated, maybe even a little confusing. We see good people, very good people, trying their best to do the right thing, but things don't always go according to plan.

Let's see if we can make some sense of all this.

Being Yourself

If you have an older brother or sister, how many times have people said to you, "Oh, you're so-and-so's younger sibling?" Or maybe you're always hearing, "You're so-and-so's daughter (or son). Nice to meet you."

And how many times did you want to answer them by saying, "Yes, that's true, but I am also *me*!"

If you have ever felt that way, you can perhaps understand the challenges Isaac faces as the son of Abraham. Abraham, who as a young child figured out that idols were silly and that there had to be one, true God. Abraham, to whom God promised the land of Israel, saying that He would be his God and the God of his descendants. Abraham, who God says will become a great nation. Abraham, a man so great that all the nations of the earth will want their children to be like him.

Is it any wonder that people often think of Isaac as the son of Abraham?

Of course, Isaac doesn't make things any easier by often copying his father, like when he says that his wife is his sister or digs wells and uses the same names for them that his father used. Still, Isaac is able to build his own reputation and his own identity. As a farmer, he is so successful that he has many, many sheep and cattle. He becomes very rich—so rich that the Philistines envy him. They even come to him and say, "We now see plainly that the LORD has been with you, and we thought: Let there be a sworn treaty between our two parties, between you and us. Let us make a pact with you."

Most important of all, God sees Isaac for who he is and not just as Abraham's son. This is why God promises Isaac that He will make Isaac's descendants as numerous as the stars of heaven. God also tells Isaac that He will give the land of Israel to his descendants "so that all the nations of the earth shall bless themselves by your heirs."

What can those of us with older brothers and sisters or famous parents learn from this? We see that Isaac is very proud to be the son of Abraham, even if it means that sometimes (maybe most of the time) people think of him as Abraham's son. He learns from his father. He even copies some things his father does. But in the end,

Toldot (Gen 25:19–28:9)

Isaac understands that he is his own person. He figures out how to do things his way, so that people in the end see him not just as Abraham's son but as Isaac, the son of Abraham.

It may be hard at times, but making a name for ourselves is important. Maybe you play the violin just like your brother does. Maybe you are a soccer star just like your sister. But just because you like the same things they do doesn't mean that you can't accomplish great things on your own. Just like Isaac.

> *Suppose you and your siblings like the same thing, whether it's sports or music or computer games. If you enjoy this activity, does it really matter if your brother or sister is better at it?*

The Importance of Talking to Friends and Family

We all have times when we don't feel like talking to our family or friends. Sometimes we're scared or nervous, and that makes us a little shy about sharing our feelings. Other times we're sad and just don't know why. There are even times when we've done something really great but are quiet about it because we don't want our friends to think we're bragging too much.

All this is normal and makes sense, but it's usually better to be open and honest with our friends and families. Why? *Toldot* gives us a good example of what can happen when people stop talking to one another.

There is no doubt that Isaac and Rebekah love each other very much. The stories about them in Genesis make this clear. However, they don't seem able to talk about things and be honest with each other.

This starts during Rebekah's pregnancy. We know that she waits a long time to become pregnant, just as we know that she has a difficult pregnancy. God explains why her pregnancy is so difficult: The twin boys she is carrying will grow up to start two very different nations. One will be mightier than the other, and when the descendants of the younger son (Jacob) act properly, they will rule over the descendants of the older son (Esau).

Just stop and think about this. God Himself explains to Rebekah what is going on with her pregnancy. He explains the cause of her difficulties and outlines the future not only of her children but of their descendants as well. And what does she do with this remarkable news? She keeps it to herself. Nowhere do we read that Rebekah shares or even hints about it to Isaac.

Why doesn't she share this exciting news with Isaac? Maybe it's the 27-year age difference between them. Isaac is 40 when they marry, and she, according to most opinions, is only 13. Maybe it's their different upbringings. Isaac is raised by Abraham and Sarah, who commit their lives to teaching others about the one, true God. As for Rebekah, she grows up among idol worshippers in a family lacking in honesty, something we will see very clearly in a few weeks, when we read about how her brother Laban treats her son Jacob.

We don't really know why Rebekah and Isaac don't seem to share important news with each other, but we do know that things get worse. When the time comes for Isaac to bless his sons, when he must choose which son will get the birthright and become leader of their family, does Isaac discuss his choice or the reasons for his choice with Rebekah? No! He doesn't even tell her about what he is going to do. She is actually forced to eavesdrop in order to know that Isaac is going to bless Esau. And because Isaac doesn't discuss any of this with Rebekah, she has no chance to tell him how she feels about their sons and his choice.

Without a chance to share her feelings with Isaac, Rebekah believes she has only one option left: to trick her husband by making Jacob pretend to be Esau. Why would she do this? In order to make God's prophecy about the younger son ruling over the older son come true (a prophecy she never shared with her husband!).

We, of course, know how the story turns out. Whatever sibling rivalry there already was between Esau and Jacob only gets worse. Jacob must run away because of his brother's anger. He must go live with his uncle Laban. Rebekah tells Jacob to stay long enough for Esau to calm down and maybe even forgive him. "How long can that take?" she must be thinking to herself. "A few months? Maybe a year or two?" She has no way of knowing that it will take 22 years.

Toldot (Gen 25:19–28:9)

And sadly, Rebekah never sees her favored son again. She dies while Jacob is away.

This is a very sad ending to the story. But the Torah isn't telling us this story because our own stories will end up just as sad if we don't talk with our friends and family and share our feelings. Instead, the Torah is making this point: Not talking with others, not sharing our feelings with others, can make our lives very, very complicated. There will be times when you will want or need to keep your feelings to yourself, but more often than not, sharing your feelings and talking with others will make things better.

Who do you turn to when you need to share your feelings? A friend? A sibling? One of your parents? Why this person?

Sibling Rivalry

There are many places where we could talk about sibling rivalry, which seems to be everywhere in the book of Genesis.

We read that Cain was so hurt and so jealous that God accepted Abel's sacrifice (and not his) that he killed his brother. Ishmael was sent away so he wouldn't be a bad influence on his brother Isaac. As we'll read later, Joseph's brothers are so jealous of him that they want to kill him. And we shouldn't forget the rivalry between Rachel and Leah, although they never threaten to kill each other.

These stories have lots going on in them. We see immature people, like Joseph, who is shown to be very childish at the beginning of his story. We have people who are afraid, like Leah, who thinks she will be forced to marry Esau. Sometimes there's no good reason for brothers not to get along, like Cain and Abel. God tells Cain to try harder and make his next sacrifice better. He kills Abel instead.

Then we have Jacob and Esau.

Maybe they're jealous of each other. Maybe they just don't like each other. But the truth is, as the midrash tells us, they're already fighting when they're in their mother's belly. It seems that their fights and struggles are all about who will be in charge, about who will take over from Isaac and Rebekah to teach the world about the one, true God. Of course, having parents who each favor one son over the other doesn't help matters.

What the Torah is trying to teach us with these stories of siblings not getting along is pretty simple: sibling rivalry is just a part of life.

Consider this: Studies have found that siblings aged seven and under fight about three to seven times an hour.[1] An hour! And it doesn't end as they get older, because an older child will often resent the younger one for getting away with more, for being given more, and for being allowed to do more at an earlier age than the older child was allowed to do.

So why does the Torah spend so much time telling us about something that is so obviously true? To answer this, you need only look at the end of all these stories. Ishmael and Isaac make up and reunite to bury their father in Hebron. Jacob and Esau hug each other and cry when they are reunited after 22 years. In the end, when they go down to Egypt, the brothers beg Joseph's forgiveness, and he cries at the idea that they would think he could stay angry at them.

Yes, says the Torah, siblings often don't get along, but in the end, their love for each other is stronger. Cain is the only brother whose anger and jealousy is stronger than his love for his sibling. And what happens to him? He is cursed by God and marked for life. He is no longer able to farm the land and spends the rest of his life as a "fugitive and wanderer."

> *Think of a time you and one of your siblings got into an argument. Not just any argument, but a really big one. Did you stay mad at each other for a long time? Why or why not? What did you do to make up? How did you feel when you made up?*

---

1. K. J. Dell'antonia, "Why Siblings Fight," *New York Times*, July 8, 2018.

Vayetze

(Gen 28:10–32:3)

TRICKS AND MORE TRICKS

Summary of This Week's Reading

As we read last week, Jacob must leave his home because of his brother's anger over Isaac's blessing. Vayetze begins with Jacob setting out on his journey to Haran, where his mother's family lives. He arrives at "the place." (The Torah doesn't give this place a name, but the rabbis identify it as Mount Moriah, the exact spot where Abraham was prepared to offer Isaac as a sacrifice and the same spot where the holy Temple would be eventually be built by King Solomon.)

Jacob decides to sleep there, and that night, he has an amazing dream: He sees a ladder that reaches from earth all the way to heaven and angels going up and down it. What's more, God appears at the top of the ladder and promises Jacob that the land on which he lies will be given to his descendants. In the morning, Jacob awakes and is frightened by his dream and by the fact he didn't realize that God was in "the place." Jacob calls the place Beth-El, which means "the house of God."

Once he arrives in Haran, Jacob meets Laban's youngest daughter, Rachel, by a well where she has come to water the sheep she is watching for her father. Jacob introduces himself to his cousin, and she brings him to her home. Jacob very quickly falls deeply in love with Rachel, and he tells Laban that he will work for him for seven years if he agrees to let him marry Rachel. Laban agrees, but, as we see throughout Vayetze, Laban isn't very honest.

Jacob works seven years, as he promised. At the end of the seven years, he tells Laban that he is ready to marry Rachel, just as they agreed. But Laban decides to trick Jacob, and on the night of the wedding, he gives Jacob his oldest daughter, Leah, in place of Rachel. (Why Jacob didn't know that it was Leah he was marrying is a great question. There is no logical answer other than that this was God's plan. For whatever reason, God clearly wanted Jacob to marry Leah first and only then marry Rachel.)

In the morning, Jacob is shocked that he has been tricked. "Why did you do this to me?" Jacob says angrily. "Did I not work seven years, just as I promised, in order to marry Rachel?" Laban simply answers Jacob that "it is not our custom for the younger sister to get married first!" Left with no other option, Jacob agrees to work for Laban another seven years in order to marry Rachel.

Vayetze goes on to tell us that Jacob and his wives start a family. Leah gives birth to six sons and a daughter, but Rachel is unable to have children. She feels a little jealous of her sister and the children she has. So just as Sarah gave her servant Hagar to Abraham, Rachel gives Jacob her servant Bilhah as a wife to have children for her. Bilhah soon has two sons.

By this time, Leah has stopped having children, but she, too, feels jealous of her sister. So Leah does the same thing Rachel did. She gives her servant Zilpah to Jacob as a wife to have children for her. Like Bilhah, Zilpah gives birth to two sons.

During all this, Rachel has been praying and praying to God to have children of her own. Her prayers are finally answered, and she gives birth to Joseph.

After 11 sons, one daughter, and 14 long years of working for Laban, Jacob is ready to return home. But Laban doesn't want to lose his best worker, so he offers to pay Jacob to keep working for him. (Always the tricky one, Laban keeps changing the deal he makes with Jacob about how he should be paid.)

Vayetze (Gen 28:10–32:3)

After six more years of Laban's trickery, Jacob decides that it's time to leave, but he is afraid that Laban will try to stop him. Jacob and his family leave in the middle of the night, when Laban is out in the fields working with his own sheep.

When Laban learns that Jacob has left with his family, he chases them. He wants to keep Jacob from leaving. But God appears to Laban in a dream and warns him not to harm Jacob. Laban listens to God, and when he finally catches up to Jacob, the two of them make a deal. Neither will bother the other ever again. Jacob gives the place where they make this deal a special name, Gal-Ed, which means "a mound that is a witness between me and you."

Jacob then continues his travels with his family. When he arrives back in Canaan, he is met by an angel. Once again, Jacob gives the place where something special happens to him a special name. He sees that "this is the camp of God," and he names the place Mahanaim, a name that means "two camps," that is, one for Jacob and one for God.

Life Lessons from Vayetze

Vayetze would make a great script for a movie. There's a hero, Jacob. A love interest, Rachel. One who loves deeply but whose love is never fully returned, Leah. A villain, Laban. Suspense. (When will he figure out he's been tricked? How will they safely escape?) Wondrous dreams. An apparently happy ending.

And, of course, some important life lessons for us.

"The Lord is in This Place, and I Did Not Know It"

Each of the patriarchs and matriarchs has a special relationship with God. Sometimes He appears to them in visions, sometimes in dreams. He speaks with them and tells them what to do ("Leave your birthplace and go to the land I will show you") and what not to do ("Do not go down to Egypt like your father did"). He even pays a visit to Abraham after his circumcision to see how he's feeling!

How, then, could Jacob come to "the place" and not know that God is there? Doesn't Jacob understand that God is everywhere?

More important, what is the Torah trying to teach us by sharing this story with us?

It may be that it is all a matter of expectations. If God appears to a person in a dream or a vision (like he did with the patriarchs and matriarchs), perhaps that person comes to believe that this is the only way God will appear. If a person worships God by building an altar (like Abraham, Isaac, and Jacob each did), maybe the person believes that you can only meet God at an altar.

Not convinced? Think about your family and friends. How many of them believe that a house of worship (like a synagogue or a church) is the only place a person can meet and speak with God? Probably a lot of them!

This is the point of Jacob coming to "the place" and not knowing that God is there. The Torah wants to remind us that God is everywhere, even in places we least expect to find Him.

Consider this example: Azaleas are very popular among serious gardeners and have been for hundreds of years. There are actually more than 10,000 varieties of azaleas, each producing flowers with incredibly vivid colors. But here's the thing about azaleas: During the winter months, they look quite lifeless. Come the spring, they seem to explode back to life, and for several weeks, their colors are remarkably beautiful. A horticulturist, a person who is an expert in plant science and care, could explain exactly how this whole process works. However, there are some people who look at their azalea plants and see God. Who but God can make a plant seem so dead in the winter and yet so alive and beautiful in the spring?

This is the challenge we all face, and this is what the story of Jacob and "the place" is teaching us. God is there, even when you don't realize it. You just have to pay better attention and look a little harder to see Him. When you do, you will come to understand that He is there, in every aspect of our lives.

> *Do you have a special place or a special activity that helps you feel close to God? What makes it so special?*

Vayetze (Gen 28:10–32:3)

Things Can't Get Worse, Can They?

Imagine that it's the start of a new school year, and you're really excited about it until the first day of school. When you get to your classroom, you learn that your best friend, who's been in your class for the past three years, will be in a different class with a different teacher. Oh no!

What's worse, you find out that you have Mr. Grumpyface (that's not his real name, but that's what everyone calls him, at least in their heads) as a math teacher. He's the hardest and meanest math teacher in the school. Oh no!

Things can't get any worse, you think. But what are you going to do about it?

Vayetze has a similar story, about a person (Leah) who thinks things can't get any worse for her, but with some patience and some hard work, things do get better. Let's take a closer look at Leah's story.

Remember that Laban tricks Jacob on his wedding night. Jacob thinks he's getting married to Rachel, but in the end, it's Leah. In the morning, Jacob is very, very angry with Laban for tricking him, but he isn't too happy with Leah, either. In fact, the Torah says, he hates her! (Many English translations of this story say that Jacob loves Leah less than Rachel. That's a nice thought, but the Hebrew says clearly that he hates her, at least at first.)

Poor Leah. She doesn't want to trick Jacob, but her father forces her to. She really does love Jacob, and now he hates her. What can she do?

It must have been hard, but she reminds Jacob that they are now married. She also reminds him that God wants him to have lots of sons, 12 to be exact, so that the Jewish people can be built from his family. Jacob may be upset, but he understands God's plan.

As it turns out, Jacob's favorite wife, Rachel, isn't able to have children for a long time. Leah, with whom he is so angry, can. And the names she picks for each of her sons gives us a hint about how her situation improves over time.

She names her first son Reuben, which comes from the Hebrew word that means "to see." Leah thinks that everyone can see how Jacob is upset with her and how he loves Rachel more than her.

She calls her second son Simeon, which comes from the Hebrew word that means "to hear." In choosing this name, she says that God heard she was unloved, so He blessed her with a second son. What's more, while others no longer see that Jacob treats her differently from Rachel, Leah still hears in his voice that he loves Rachel more.

Leah names her third son Levi, which comes from the Hebrew word that means "to lend something." You must trust and have good relations with another person to lend him or her something. Leah picks this name because she feels, after her third child, that Jacob trusts her and has become attached to her.

Leah has a fourth son, and she calls him Judah, which comes from the Hebrew word that means "to praise." She praises and thanks God because with this fourth child, it is clear to all that Jacob has come to love her.

It wasn't easy, and it took a long time, but Leah was able to make things better for herself (and for Jacob, too). And that's the lesson we should take from this story. Not every real-life story has a happy ending, but Leah's story is here to remind us to be hopeful and to be patient. Things usually have a way of working themselves out.

> Like many of us, you have probably had times when things just didn't seem to be going well for you. What did you do to try and make things better? Did it work? If so, how?

Taking Your Responsibilities Seriously

There is no doubt that Laban treats Jacob very badly. He starts by tricking Jacob into marrying Leah instead of Rachel. He gives Jacob food and a place to live for 14 years but doesn't pay him for the work he does. (Jacob's "salary" was being allowed to marry Laban's two daughters.) Once Jacob threatens to leave, Laban agrees to pay him for his work. But, of course, Laban immediately tries to trick Jacob. At first, Laban agrees to pay Jacob with spotted sheep.

Then Laban changes the deal to speckled sheep. And, finally, he changes it to striped sheep.

Would anyone blame Jacob for not working hard? Or for playing "hooky" occasionally? Yet Jacob does no such thing. He works very hard, day in and day out. Sometimes he goes nights without sleeping to be sure the sheep he is supposed to watch are safe. And if a wild animal comes and kills one of the sheep, Jacob pays for the dead sheep himself, even though it wasn't his fault.

This is why Jacob is such a good worker—actually, the best worker that Laban has. He takes his job and his responsibilities very seriously, even though Laban is a bad boss and an even worse person. Jacob understands that when a person takes on a job, he or she has a responsibility to do the best job possible.

What do we learn from this? That we can only control what we do and make sure we always do our best. We can't control what other people choose to do or not to do. Jacob can't make Laban a better boss. He can only make himself the best shepherd he can be!

> *Do you have a regular job or chore to do at home or at school? Are you good at it? Did you have to work at becoming good at it? What made you want to be good at it?*

Vayishlach

(Gen 32:4–36:43)

PART ONE—DO WE BELIEVE IN ANGELS?

At first glance, the main characters of this week's reading would seem to be Jacob and Esau. After all, they are meeting each other again after being apart for more than 20 years! But, as we will soon see, this reading features other important characters: angels.

At the beginning of our story, it seems that Jacob sends angels ahead of him to meet Esau. And while later in the story the verses describe Jacob wresting with a man until dawn, Jewish tradition is very clear that this is no man but rather an angel. What's more, this isn't the first story to feature angels. If you remember, angels came to visit Abraham to tell him that he and Sarah would soon have a son. These same angels continued on to Sodom to destroy the city and to save Lot. An angel came to Hagar and showed her a well when her son Ishmael was near death because he had no water to drink. An angel called out to Abraham to stop him from actually sacrificing Isaac.

We believe in angels because Genesis seems to be filled with angels. But what exactly are angels?

Let's start with what they're not. Unlike what you may have seen on TV shows or in movies or even in cartoons, the angels we believe in don't look like people dressed in white robes, with wings and halos, who often spend their time playing a harp.

The best hint at what angels really are comes from the Hebrew word for angel: *malach*. Sometimes this word is translated "angel," and sometimes it is translated "messenger." In other words, angels are messengers sent by God on various missions, and every angel is "programmed" to perform a specific task. The angels who visited Abraham were programmed to tell him he would soon have a son. The angel who appeared to Hagar was programmed to show her where to find water to save her son. The angel Jacob wrestles with in this week's reading was programmed to give him a new name. And because these angels meet with and speak to (and sometimes wrestle with) human beings, God gives them human forms, so as not to shock or scare the people they meet.

Perhaps you're wondering why God Himself doesn't deliver these messages. That's a good question.

We see in Genesis that God does appear in visions or dreams to the most special of people and with the most special of messages. For instance, God appears to Abraham to tell him that he and his descendants will become a great nation and that He will always be their God. God also appears to Isaac to tell him not to go down to Egypt and to remind him that He, God, will always be with him. God adds that He will bless him and that He will give the land of Israel to his children, just as He promised Abraham. Finally, God appears to Jacob and makes this promise to him: "Your descendants shall be as the dust of the earth; you shall spread out to the west and to the east, to the north and to the south. All the families of the earth shall bless themselves by you and your descendants."

We can all understand how special these messages are, because they're about things that affect the entire Jewish people. That is why God Himself wanted to deliver them. But not every story in Genesis is about something very special. There are many stories about regular life: about things like getting married and having children, or even going to work every day. Yet sometimes during their regular daily lives, the characters in Genesis get messages from God, and for these important but less special messages, God sends angels as messengers. The messages delivered by angels include telling

Vayishlach (Gen 32:4–36:43)

Abraham that he will have a son, which is important but not so special. (After all, lots of people have children.) Or showing Hagar where to find water, which is important, but in those days, people dug wells to find water all the time. Or giving Jacob a new name, which may turn out to be important, but, then again, many people change their names.

In the end, it may be that God only delivers messages Himself that affect the Jewish nation as a whole. At least, that seems to be the pattern in Genesis.

And what about today? Why don't we see angels in our times? Does God not have messages for us as a people? These are great questions. They are hard questions. Here is one possible answer:

In Genesis, the Jewish people are not yet a great nation. They are a family, one that grows larger from generation to generation, but still only a family. In those times, a single person, like Abraham or Sarah or the other patriarchs and matriarchs, could make decisions for the family that had an impact on everyone. Today, depending on whom you ask, there are approximately 15 to 20 million Jews in the world. And no one in is a position to speak for all of us or to make decisions for all of us. Maybe that's why we don't hear from or see angels today.

Or maybe, in our times, there are no people as great or as special as the patriarchs and matriarchs.

Or maybe, as we noted earlier in this book, some questions are simply better than any answer we might come up with for them.

Whichever answer you prefer, this is a topic worth thinking about.

Vayishlach

(Gen 32:4–36:43)

PART TWO—BROTHERS REUNITED

Summary of This Week's Reading

After a 20-year stay in Haran, Jacob is finally heading home, back to Canaan. He knows he will meet Esau along the way but is unsure of whether Esau is still angry about their father's blessing. Jacob sends messengers (who may actually be angels) ahead to Esau, hoping to make peace with him. But the messengers return and tell Jacob that Esau is coming to fight him with 400 armed men. (Some scholars think these were 400 generals, each commanding 400 armed men!) Jacob knows what he must do. He prepares for war by dividing his wives and children into two camps; he prays to God for help; and he sends Esau many gifts, with the hope that these gifts will make Esau less angry and more forgiving.

The night before he is to meet Esau, Jacob takes his family and all their possessions across the Jabbok River. He, however, remains behind. (It is not clear why he does this. Some think he crossed back over the river to be sure nothing important was left behind.) Jacob meets what he thinks is a man and what we know to be an angel. This angel is a kind of defender of Esau, and the angel therefore starts wrestling

VAYISHLACH (GEN 32:4–36:43)

with Jacob. Neither the angel nor Jacob can defeat the other (although the angel does hurt Jacob's hip), and their struggle goes on all night.

As sunrise draws near, the angel begs Jacob to let him go. Jacob agrees, but only on the condition that the angel bless him. So, the angel blesses him and gives him a new name: "Your name shall no longer be Jacob, but Israel, for you have striven [or fought] with beings divine and human, and have prevailed [or won]."

Later that day, Jacob and Esau meet. They hug and kiss. (We will talk more about this shortly.) Then they go their separate ways.

When Jacob reaches Canaan, he buys some land near the town of Shechem. The prince of this town—who is also called Shechem—kidnaps Jacob's daughter, Dinah. Dinah's brothers Simeon and Levi rescue her.

Jacob's journey, however, is not over, because he has not yet arrived home to see his father. While he and his family are traveling, Rachel gives birth to her second son, Benjamin, but it is a difficult birth, and she dies. Jacob, who is very, very sad, buries her in a roadside grave near Bethlehem.

At this point in the story, the midrash comes along to fill in some details. It says that after Rachel dies, Jacob must decide which of his wives he will now spend most of his time with. He chooses Rachel's servant Bilhah, because she had been helping raise his son Joseph and would help take care of the new baby. This bothers Reuben, Leah's oldest son. He thinks Jacob should be spending most of his time with his mother, Leah, who was, along with Rachel, one of Jacob's main wives. Reuben even goes so far as to put Jacob's bed in Leah's tent. (Each of Jacob's wives has her own tent.) Jacob is not happy with Reuben's actions.

Jacob finally arrives at his parents' home in Hebron. Isaac is still alive and lives to be 180. Sadly, Rebekah died before Jacob was able to return home.

This reading concludes with a detailed account (an entire chapter in the Torah!) of Esau's wives, children, and grandchildren, including the family histories of the people of Seir, among whom Esau settles, and a list of the eight kings who rule Edom, the land of Esau's and Seir's descendants. (We will talk more about why we need to know all these details about Esau and his family next week.)

Life Lessons from Vayishlach

Every Day is a New Day

How often do you and your friends argue over who or what is the greatest of all time? Maybe it's sports. (Lebron James or Michael Jordan?) Maybe it's flavors of ice cream. (Chocolate or vanilla? Neither. It's actually Ben and Jerry's New York Super Fudge Chunk.) Maybe it's even presidents of the United States. (Washington or Lincoln?)

Sometimes people have a similar debate about the patriarchs. Was Abraham greater than Isaac? Was Isaac greater than Jacob? The truth is, each was a remarkable and extraordinary person. Each had character traits or good deeds that made him different, but no less great, than the other two. For Jacob, it was having 12 righteous sons who would each go on to be the head of one of Israel's 12 tribes.

You may be asking, what does all this have to do with this week's reading? The answer is simple. After being apart from his brother for more than 20 years, Jacob is about to meet Esau, and he's not sure if Esau is still angry about their father's blessing. When Jacob last saw Esau, Esau wanted to kill him. Does he still want to kill him?

It's not surprising that Jacob is a little nervous, nor is it surprising that he would pray to God to ask for help. What is surprising is Jacob's prayer: "I am unworthy of all the kindness that You have so steadfastly shown Your servant."

Wait a minute. How can Jacob, one of the three patriarchs and the father of the 12 tribes of Israel, be unworthy? If Jacob isn't worthy, who among us is?

Here's the point Jacob is making: He knows that he has done many great things in his life and that he has served God the best he could for many, many years. But Jacob understands that the great things he did yesterday or last week or last year won't help him today. Today is a new day, and each new day means that he must work hard to do great things and to serve God. Jacob thinks he's unworthy because he's not sure whether he's acted in a way that makes today a great and special day.

Vayishlach (Gen 32:4–36:43)

If you can remember this lesson and treat each day as a new opportunity for doing special things for your family, your friends, and God, each day will be a great day and will go far in making you worthy in the eyes of God.

> *Given that every day is a new day, what can you do today that's special? What will you do on the Sabbath? Next week? At home? In school? For your friends?*

Doing All We Can

It shouldn't be surprising that Jacob prays to God for help with his meeting with Esau. Prayer was a regular part of Jacob's life, just as it is for many people today. But Jacob doesn't rely only on prayer, and the actions he takes teach us another important lesson.

As important as prayer is, as much as he needs and hopes for God's help, Jacob knows that he has to do his part, too. He has to do all he can to help himself, even as he prays to God for help.

What does Jacob do? He sends seven messengers to greet Esau, each bearing many gifts. Jacob hopes that the gifts will show Esau how sorry he is, and maybe, just maybe, make Esau less angry.

Jacob also divides his family and all the animals he owns into two groups. He does this just in case his prayers and his gifts don't work. If Esau were to attack one of the groups, the other would be able to escape.

Yes, doing all he can includes prayer. But with the gifts he sends and the actions he takes in case he must fight Esau, Jacob reminds us that we must always do everything we can to help ourselves in difficult times, whether we're preparing for an upcoming test at school or an equally challenging problem outside of school. As Benjamin Franklin wrote in the 1757 edition of his *Poor Richard's Almanac*, "God helps them that help themselves."

> *Can you remember a time when you had to do two or three things at the same time to achieve your goal? How did it make you feel in the end? Did you think you were really doing all you could?*

Judging People Favorably

There some very specific rules when it comes to writing a Torah scroll. For example, there are no commas or periods or any other kind of punctuation at all. There are no lowercase or capital letters. There are no paragraph breaks. But there are some exceptions to these rules. We do occasionally find an oversized letter or an extra small letter. And when we come across these exceptions, the rabbis always give an explanation. One of the biggest exceptions is found in this week's reading.

Imagine this scene: It has been more than 20 years since Esau last saw Jacob. And now, when he sees Jacob, he runs toward his brother. Then the verse continues: "He embraced him and, falling on his neck, he kissed him; and they wept." What a sight that must have been! Could the verse have been any clearer about how thrilled Esau was to see Jacob after so long?

Actually, yes, it could have been clearer, and here's why. If you look at the image below, you will see that the Hebrew word for "he kissed him" has a dot over each of the letters. This is very unusual, because, as we have said, a Torah scroll generally has no punctuation at all.

For the rabbis, these dots are a signal that there is more to the phrase "he kissed him" than we may have thought. Remember that up to this point in our story, Esau has usually been portrayed as a mean, scary guy. Would such a person really fall on his brother's neck, hugging and kissing him?

There are many who would say, no, Esau would not act in such a way. They insist that Esau is really trying to trick Jacob. According to this version of the story (found in the Jewish oral tradition), Esau pretends to cry, and when he hugs Jacob, he tries to bite his

Vayishlach (Gen 32:4–36:43)

neck! God performs a miracle and turns Jacob's neck to stone. Esau breaks his teeth, and Jacob is saved.

This is the version of the story taught to most children. Why? Because people don't want to give Esau the benefit of the doubt. It is true that he isn't the nicest of people, but people do change. And even if Esau hasn't really changed, it is still possible that at that moment, he was truly overcome with emotion, that he was happy to the point of tears to see his brother again.

The truth is, the Jewish oral tradition also has this version of the story. In fact, the great Bible commentator Rabbi Shlomo Yitzhaki, known as Rashi, includes both versions of the story in his commentary. Why? Because Rashi understands the importance of giving people the benefit of the doubt. It may be easy and even natural to see Esau as a bad person who wants to bite his brother's neck. And that's what the dots are there to do: to remind us that this is one way to look at Esau. But the dots, as Rashi understands, should also remind us there are often two sides to a story. When there are, it is important to always look for the positive and to always give others the benefit of the doubt.

> *Why do you think it's so hard to give others the benefit of the doubt? Can you think of things you can do to be sure to see the positive in others and always give them the benefit of the doubt?*

Vayeshev

(Gen 37:1–40:23)

PART ONE—WHAT'S UP WITH THE JOSEPH STORY?

This week's reading marks the beginning of one of Genesis's longest and, dare we say, craziest stories. Picture the scene: A family with 12 brothers, all of whom are shepherds. The second youngest, Joseph, is in his teens. He is Daddy's favorite, which annoys his brothers, because Daddy doesn't hide who his favorite is. Besides being pampered, Joseph is very immature and a tattletale to boot, which further annoys his brothers.

Because he is so immature and because he is used to being given special treatment, Joseph doesn't notice how annoyed his brothers are with him. So, of course, when he has not one but two dreams about becoming the head of the family and ruling over his brothers, he tells his brothers all about the dreams. The brothers are now beyond annoyed. They want to kill him, not just in theory or in their imaginations, but in real life. Fortunately, the oldest of the brothers calms everyone down. They don't kill the annoying little brother; they just sell him as a slave.

And so, the annoying little brother ends up in Egypt. He works as a slave for a year, but his master's wife falls in love with him. Not good. When she tries to kiss him, he runs away. This embarrasses her and makes her angry. She tells her husband that the slave actually tried to kiss her instead, and the annoying little brother ends up in prison.

Fast forward ten years. Joseph, the annoying little brother, is now a grown man, when he finds himself sharing a cell with two of the king's top advisors. They are in prison because they did some silly, careless things that angered the king. (And what did kings do in the old days when they were angry with someone? They sent them to prison.) These two men have dreams they can't explain or understand. Joseph interprets their dreams, and his interpretations prove correct. One man is set free from prison, and the other is hanged.

Are you following all this?

Two more years pass, and Joseph is now 30 years old. The king has a dream that scares him. He wants to know what it means, but none of his advisors understand the dream either. Suddenly, the one who was in prison remembers that the annoying little brother/grown man correctly interpreted his dream. The king sends for this man, who promptly tells the king just what his dream means and just what the king must do to prevent the bad things in the dream from coming true.

What does the king do? He takes the advice of this man he just released from prison and then makes him ruler of Egypt (second only to the king himself).

Okay, this is what we have: A 17-year-old shepherd is sold as a slave, spends a year as a slave, spends 12 years in prison, and then is suddenly made ruler of the most powerful kingdom of his time. Things like this don't really happen, do they? Maybe not in our times, but this is exactly what happens to Joseph, Jacob's favorite son.

So, what's with this story? Why does God do so many crazy things to Joseph?

To answer this question, we need to go back to Abraham and the frightening vision God shared with him about the future of his descendants. If you remember, God tells Abraham that his descendants will live in a land that is not theirs and that they will be made

VAYESHEV (GEN 37:1–40:23)

slaves by a foreign king. This, of course, isn't the type of news you keep to yourself. Abraham surely shared it with Isaac, and Isaac in turn shared it with Jacob.

Now let's see what this has to do with Joseph.

Before Joseph's brothers sold him into slavery, Jacob had had a difficult life. He had to flee from his brother Esau, who wanted to kill him. He worked for 20 long years for Laban, who tricked him and tried to cheat him over and over. When Jacob was finally able to return home, his beloved wife Rachel died along the way after giving birth to Benjamin. And once Jacob reached home and arrived back in the land of Canaan, his daughter, Dinah, was kidnapped. (She was rescued by her brothers Simeon and Levi, but it was a messy situation.)

It seems that by now, things have quieted down, and Jacob is looking forward to a quiet, uneventful life. Do you really think he wants to tell his family that they need to move to Egypt, where they will eventually end up being slaves? Of course not. But what Jacob wants and what God wants aren't the same. God has decided that Jacob and his family must go down to Egypt. In fact, according to the midrash, God is so determined for Jacob go down to Egypt that He is prepared to send angels to drag Jacob down there in chains!

In the end, God has a better idea, and that better idea is the story of Joseph. As we work our way through the story, crazy as it might seem, we will see that in the end, Jacob must bring his family to Egypt (because of a famine) and that he will want to go down to Egypt (to see Joseph again). And with Joseph as the ruler of Egypt, Jacob himself will be treated with great honor and dignity, even if his descendants end up as slaves after he dies.

There is one other important fact to keep in mind about the Joseph story. It seems so unbelievable that the hand of God must have been behind it every step of the way.

Perhaps all this makes clear what's up with the Joseph story, but it probably leaves you with another unanswered question: why would God want to make Jacob and his descendants slaves in the first place? This is exactly the type of question we've mentioned before: a question that's better than the answers we can uncover.

With that said, let's see if we can explain why the Jews were made slaves in Egypt.

When Jacob relocates to Egypt, he brings with him his wives, children, and grandchildren, and when Joseph and his family (who are already in Egypt) are added to the count, they add up to 70 people. What happens to these individuals and their families during the long years of slavery?

First, they increase in number, and not just by a little but by a lot. The Egyptians are afraid of the Jews, and they try to keep the Jewish women from having any babies. But God has other plans. The Jewish women have lots and lots and lots of babies. So many, in fact, that when Moses first counts the people who leave Egypt with him, there are more than 600,000 men between the ages of 20 and 60. (Moses was only counting the men who could serve in the army.) If we take into account their wives, the children younger than 20, and the adults older than 60, there were probably two to three million people who left Egypt.

Second, the Egyptians, like many others over the centuries, try to make the Jews less Jewish. The midrash tells us how. The Egyptians want the Jews to stop speaking Hebrew and to stop giving their children Hebrew names. But Jacob's descendants refuse. Not only do they keep speaking Hebrew and keep using Hebrew names, they also refuse to wear Egyptian clothing. Instead, they continue to dress as they had when they lived in Canaan. This means that even the clothes they wear let others know that they're Jewish. So, instead of making them less Jewish, the Egyptians make the Jews more Jewish.

Third, the Egyptians, especially their king, Pharaoh, think that if they make the lives of the Jews particularly miserable, the Jews will stop believing in God. But they're wrong. The worse the Egyptians make their lives, the more the Jews cry out to God and ask Him to save them. In the end, the rabbis teach, it is their strong faith in God that compels Him to bring the Jews out of Egypt.

In other words, the Jews go down to Egypt simply as a family. Many, many years later, when God tells Moses to bring the Jews out of Egypt, they leave not as a family but as a nation. And not just

VAYESHEV (GEN 37:1–40:23)

any nation but one great enough and with enough faith in God to receive His commandments and become His special people.

Were there not other ways for God to turn Jacob's family into a great nation? Sure there were, but for reasons only He understands, God thought that being slaves in Egypt was the best way to make this happen.

Whether you understand or even like this answer, one thing is clear: it did work, and the Jewish people remain a great nation to this very day.

Vayeshev

(Gen 37:1–40:23)

PART TWO—THE LONG, TWISTED TALE BEGINS

Summary of This Week's Reading

Jacob is relieved that his reunion with Esau was short and uneventful. Now that he has finally arrived back in his homeland, Jacob settles in Hebron with his family, hoping for some peace and quiet. And why not? He has had many difficult challenges in his life: having to run away from home because of Esau's anger about the blessing, dealing with Laban and all his lies, Rachel dying while giving birth to Benjamin, and the unfortunate story of Dinah and Shechem. But God has other plans, and the long, twisted tale of Jacob going down to Egypt begins.

The story opens with Jacob's favorite son, Joseph, who will be its main character. Joseph is only 17 years old when we meet him, and the truth is, he isn't very mature. Jacob favors Joseph, giving him that famous coat (whether it has many colors or not is unclear). Joseph loves being the center of attention (who wouldn't?) and seems not to notice how jealous his brothers are of him. In fact, he makes things worse over and over again. For example, when he thinks he sees his brothers doing something wrong, Joseph is quick to run to his father

Vayeshev (Gen 37:1–40:23)

to tattle on them. Unfortunately, Joseph gets his facts wrong, and his tattletales upset his brothers a lot.

Joseph then has not one but two dreams that seem to show that someday, he will be head of the family. Joseph doesn't stop to consider his brothers' feelings, and he tells them about his dreams. Not surprisingly, his brothers hate him even more because of the dreams. They hate him so much that they actually begin thinking about ways to kill him! And when Joseph goes out to the fields where the brothers are watching their father's flocks, things look bad for him. Once he arrives, Simeon and Levi are ready to kill him then and there, but Reuben suggests that they throw him into a pit instead. (He doesn't tell the other brothers, but Reuben suggests this so he can come back later to save Joseph.) While Joseph is in the pit, Judah has a great idea. Instead of killing Joseph, they should sell him as a slave to some Ishmaelite traders who happen to be passing by.

Once Joseph is gone, the brothers tear his special coat and dip it in the blood of a goat. They take it home and show it to their father. When Jacob sees it, he assumes that Joseph has been killed and eaten by a wild animal. He is sadder than the brothers ever imagined he would be. They blame Judah for this, because it was his idea to sell Joseph as a slave. And they are so angry with him that Judah has to move away from his family.

Things continue to go badly for Judah. He gets married and has three children, but his wife and two of his sons die. Judah's story then becomes even more complicated. He ends up having twins with a woman named Tamar, who had been married to both of his dead sons, one after the other. (We told you it was a complicated story.) One of the twins, Peretz, is an ancestor of King David.

The focus of the story now returns to Joseph, who is taken to Egypt and sold to Potiphar, a minister to Pharaoh, king of Egypt. God watches over Joseph and blesses everything he does. Potiphar can't help but notice this, and he puts Joseph in charge of all his property. Although he is still a slave, things seem to be looking up for Joseph until Potiphar's wife notices him. She sees how handsome Joseph is, and she keeps trying to get Joseph to kiss her. Joseph says no again and again because he knows that kissing her is very wrong, since she's married to someone else. This, of course, makes Mrs. Potiphar very angry—so angry that she lies to her husband and tells him that Joseph actually kissed her! Potiphar doesn't really believe his wife, but he has no choice but to throw Joseph in prison.

Still, God continues to watch over Joseph. Even in prison, people notice this, and again, Joseph is put in charge of things.

At this point, Joseph's story takes another twist. With him in prison are Pharaoh's chief butler and chief baker, who were both sent to prison for silly reasons. (While the text does not us the precise reasons why, the midrash says that the chief butler gave Pharaoh a cup of wine with a fly in it and the chief baker served Pharaoh a loaf of bread that had a pebble in it.) Both men have dreams on the same night that scare them very much. They tell Joseph their dreams, and he interprets them. In three days, he tells them, the butler will be freed and the baker hanged. Joseph's predictions come true, and before he goes free, Joseph asks the butler to tell Pharaoh how he, Joseph, ended up in prison and to convince Pharaoh to release him. But the butler forgets about Joseph and does nothing for him.

Life Lessons from Vayeshev

Being Sensitive to Other People's Feelings

After Rachel dies, Jacob begins to favor Joseph and to treat him differently from the other brothers. This is partly because Joseph is the oldest child of his beloved Rachel and partly because Jacob sees that Joseph is very bright and talented. Jacob spends more time with Joseph than he does with his other sons, Joseph doesn't have to work in the fields watching his father's flocks like the other brothers do, and Jacob gives Joseph that very special coat.[1]

It's hard to blame Joseph for feeling special given how special his father thinks he is. And the truth is, it's okay to feel good about

---

1. It is important to remember that it isn't clear from the story itself what made this coat so special. Many believe it was coat of many colors, but some think it was made of special fabric instead. Others think it was unique because of its long sleeves, and some even think that it wasn't a coat at all but actually a vest. No matter what it looked like, the other brothers understood that this coat was just one more way in which their father treated Joseph differently from them.

your special talents, no matter what they are. But feeling good about or even proud of things you do well doesn't mean you should ignore how your being good at something can make your family or friends feel, especially if they're not as "gifted" as you.

Being sensitive to the feelings of others requires maturity, and even though he is a teenager when this story begins, Joseph isn't very mature. He only thinks about all the special things his father does for him. He never stops to think about how his brothers feel about all of it. And as we mentioned in our summary of this week's reading, Joseph makes things worse by telling his brothers about his dreams. Had Joseph stopped and considered his brothers' feelings, he would have understood that it would have been better to keep his dreams to himself.

Who knows? Maybe if Joseph had been more sensitive to his brothers' feelings, his story would have turned out very differently. But he wasn't, and the results of his lack of sensitivity teach us a very important lesson—one that is certainly worth remembering!

> *Imagine you have a special talent or skill that you're proud of. (Maybe you do, so you don't have to imagine.) Then list some ways you can share your excitement or pride with your friends while still being respectful of their feelings.*

Thinking beyond the Here and Now

The brothers are upset with Joseph. They are angry with him because of the special treatment he receives. And when Joseph seems to brag about this special treatment by telling them about his dreams, they begin to really, really hate him.

Their hatred makes the brothers take extreme actions. Some might even call their actions crazy. After all, who sells a younger brother to be a slave? But their hatred makes them do something else, too. It makes them think only about the here and now. What do we mean by this?

Selling Joseph as a slave solves their big problem: no more hated little brother! But they never really think about the consequences of their actions. They never ask themselves how the rest of the family will feel about Joseph's disappearance, especially their father. In the end, Jacob is sadder than words can describe. He is so sad that God no longer speaks with him, and this goes on for 22 years (until he is reunited with Joseph, which we'll read about in a few weeks).

All of us face many decisions every day. Some are easy, and others are hard. Making good decisions means thinking not only about what will happen right now because of the decisions we make but also about what will happen tomorrow or next week or even next year. The brothers forget this lesson, which helps explain why this week's reading spends so much time on this part of the story. Remembering this story can help us avoid making the same mistake.

> *Have you ever made a decision that seemed like a good one at the time but turned out to be not so great? What happened in the end? Do you think this was because you didn't think ahead when making this decision? How?*

Doing the Right Thing Is Always Right, If Not Easy

Joseph may be immature, and he may sometimes use bad judgement (as he does by ignoring his brothers' feelings), but he knows right from wrong. This is something he learned from his father, Jacob, just as Jacob learned it from his father, Isaac (who, in turn, learned it from his father, Abraham). So when Mrs. Potiphar wants to kiss him, Joseph immediately knows it is wrong. He understands that kissing Mrs. Potiphar would be a betrayal of the trust his master Potiphar placed in him. Worse still, Joseph knows that doing so would be a betrayal of the God he believes in and the faith he inherited from his ancestors.

Of course, Joseph does the right thing. Of course, he says no to Mrs. Potiphar. But Mrs. Potiphar doesn't see things the same way. She sees nothing wrong in kissing Joseph, and she gets very angry when Joseph won't kiss her. And because of her anger, Joseph pays a steep price for doing the right thing: he ends up in prison for 12 long years.

The Torah is all about us doing the right thing. In its later books, it has many commandments whose purpose is to help us

Vayeshev (Gen 37:1–40:23)

see the difference between right and wrong and then to guide us in choosing to do the right thing. There are many stories in Genesis that are there for this very reason, and the story of Joseph and Mrs. Potiphar just might be the most important one of them all.

There is no way for Joseph to know that he will end up in prison for 12 years, but he realizes that trouble awaits him for doing the right thing. Joseph sees that he has a choice to make, and for him, it's an easy decision. He recognizes that a person should always do what is right, even when it's hard to do the right thing.

We all hope that it will never be hard for us to do the right thing, but when it is, it will be worthwhile to remember the example Joseph sets for us in his dealings with Mrs. Potiphar.

> *Suppose you saw a friend cheating on a test in math class. You know the right thing to do is to tell the teacher, but you also know that your friend will be angry with you if you do. What would you do? How would you explain your decision to your friend?*

Miketz

(Gen 41:1–44:17)

ONE DREAM OR TWO?

Summary of This Week's Reading

Two years have passed since Pharaoh's butler was released from prison, just as Joseph predicted. But despite his promise, the butler completely forgets about Joseph—that is, until Pharaoh has a strange and disturbing dream.[1]

What makes this dream so strange? In it, Pharaoh sees seven beautiful and healthy cows grazing by the Nile river. Then, seven thin and sickly-looking cows come up out of the Nile and eat the healthy cows. Stranger still, the sickly cows look no different after eating the healthy cows.

It gets stranger still. As the dream continues, Pharaoh sees seven full stalks of grain growing by the Nile. Then, seven dried-out, nasty looking stalks of grain pop up, and they eat the healthy stalks. (Creepy, right? How do plants eat other plants?)

---

1. Many people mistakenly believe that Pharaoh has two dreams, not one. Yet, a careful reading of the story makes it clear that it is a single dream. In fact, in his interpretation of it, Joseph says quite simply that "Pharaoh's dream is one," and Pharaoh accepts this interpretation as correct.

What makes this dream so disturbing to Pharaoh is that he senses the dream is related to him as king. But none of his wise men or magicians see the dream this way. According to the midrash, they interpret the dream as a message for Pharaoh as a person, not as the king. They tell Pharaoh things like "You will have seven sons who will die and seven daughters who will die." Pharaoh rejects such interpretations.

Suddenly, the butler remembers his dream from prison and how Joseph knew exactly what it meant. He tells Pharaoh about Joseph, and Pharaoh immediately orders that Joseph be brought to him. Pharaoh tells Joseph about his dream but leaves out certain details. Joseph tells Pharaoh that interpretations of dreams come from God, not from him. He then fills in the details Pharaoh leaves out and tells Pharaoh that the number seven in his dream represents seven years. The healthy cows and healthy stalks of grain represent seven years of plenty, years in which food will be plentiful in Egypt. The seven sickly cows and sickly stalks of grain represent seven years of famine. Why does the dream seem to repeat itself? Joseph tells Pharaoh that God will quickly make these things come to pass. What's more, the famine will be so severe that the seven years of plenty will be completely forgotten.

As soon as Pharoah hears Joseph's interpretation of his dream, he knows it to be true.

But Joseph isn't through. He goes on to offer advice to Pharaoh about how to store food during the years of plenty so that there will be food in Egypt during the seven years of famine. Pharaoh is so impressed with Joseph's proposed plan that he makes Joseph the ruler of Egypt, second only to Pharaoh himself. He instructs Joseph to carry out his plan.

At this point, Joseph marries Potiphar's daughter and has two sons. His plan is working perfectly. His life is going well. And he seems to have forgotten his father and brothers back in Canaan.

Then the years of famine come. They are difficult years in Egypt, and even worse in the countries that border Egypt, such as Canaan. Jacob and his sons run out of food because of the famine, so Jacob tells his sons to go to Egypt to buy some food for the family. (Benjamin, as Rachel's only remaining son, stays home.)

Now the story gets really interesting.

MIKETZ (GEN 41:1–44:17)

As ruler of Egypt, Joseph is in charge of selling food during the years of famine, and when his brothers arrive from Canaan to buy food, he recognizes them. What's more, he remembers the dreams he had as a teenager, dreams that suggested his brothers would bow down to him and he would be the head of the family.

Joseph doesn't reveal his true identity to his brothers, but why not? Perhaps he is still angry with his brothers (who wouldn't be?). Some suggest he is waiting to see if his dreams come true, but most believe that Joseph hides his identity in order to test his brothers to see if they've changed and if they're sorry for having sold him into slavery.

And what a test it is!

First, Joseph accuses the brothers of being spies and has them arrested. After three days, he releases them and sells them some food. But he tells them that they can't come back to Egypt to buy more food unless they bring their youngest brother, whom they left in Canaan, with them. To make sure that they do come back, Joseph has Simeon arrested and held hostage.

The brothers are both scared and confused, and they grow more so when, on their way home, they find all the money they used to buy food back in the bags on their donkeys. Now this strange ruler of Egypt will think they're thieves in addition to being spies!

When they arrive home, the brothers tell Jacob all that happened to them in Egypt. Jacob is furious. "Why did you tell them about Benjamin?" he asks. "And why would I let Benjamin go back to Egypt with you? Joseph is gone. Simeon is gone. I can't lose another son, especially the last son of my beloved Rachel."

Time passes, and the food they bought from Egypt is almost gone. They must go back to buy more, but the brothers know that without Benjamin, the suspicious Egyptian ruler won't sell them any more food. They argue with their father and beg him to change his mind. Reuben promises to protect Benjamin. Jacob isn't convinced. Only when Judah steps forward to guarantee Benjamin's safety does Jacob agree to let him go.

The brothers are very nervous when they return to Egypt. How can they explain the money they found in their bags? (They have no idea that Joseph ordered that the money be secretly returned to them before they left Egypt the first time.) To their amazement, the Egyptian ruler believes them, frees Simeon, and makes a special dinner in their honor. The next day, they buy more food and head for home.

But Joseph is far from finished with his brothers. He orders his servants to hide his special silver goblet (a fancy wine cup) in Benjamin's bag of food. After the brothers depart, his servants chase them down and accuse them of stealing the goblet. They insist that they are innocent even as they are brought back to Joseph (whom they still don't recognize as their long-lost brother). The brothers go on to say that the Egyptian ruler may kill the thief if the goblet is found in their bags. When Joseph is told of this conversation, he says that he will be merciful and will merely make the thief his slave.

The brothers, however, aren't concerned. They know they didn't steal the goblet, so imagine their shock when it's found in Benjamin's bag! And imagine how upset they are at the prospect of Benjamin remaining a slave in Egypt!

And this week's reading ends here. What a cliffhanger!

Life Lessons from Miketz

Be Proud of Who You Are

There is a very interesting and perhaps unexpected lesson to be learned from Joseph's first meeting with Pharaoh.

Pharaoh wakes from his dream, and he is frantic. He realizes that this was no ordinary dream, and he's anxious to find someone, anyone, who can interpret it for him. As he nervously asks his wise men and his magicians for their opinions, we can imagine that the butler is there, ready to serve food and drink to all who want some. Hearing these discussions, he suddenly remembers his dream. He humbly reminds Pharaoh about his time in prison and about his dream. He goes on to tell Pharaoh that there was someone in prison with him who could and did interpret it correctly. The butler is also quick to describe this person in less than complimentary terms. He calls Joseph "a young man," which may not seem like an insult, but in Egypt, young people weren't thought of as being wise. Wisdom, they thought, only came as one grew older. The butler then calls

MIKETZ (GEN 41:1–44:17)

Joseph a "Hebrew," which is what Jews were called at the time. In other words, he is saying that this interpreter of dreams rejects the religious beliefs of Egypt. Finally, he tells Pharaoh that Joseph is a "slave."

Despite all this, Pharaoh orders that Joseph be brought to him. Joseph has been in prison for 12 long years and is now being summoned by the king of the most powerful country of the time, and what does he do? Does he rush to meet the king and do as he commands? No, Joseph pauses to shower and get a haircut! What is going on here?

Joseph knows that Pharaoh has never before met a Hebrew. Joseph is proud of his culture and of his faith. He wants to make a good impression on Pharaoh, not just for himself, but for his people as well. And so, even as the guards are rushing him from prison to bring him to Pharaoh as quickly as possible, Joseph insists that he be allowed to shower and get a haircut, and to put on proper clothes as well.

Does it work? Would Pharaoh have rejected Joseph's interpretation of his dream had Joseph been dirty and dressed in prison clothes? Probably not, but being clean and properly groomed certainly helped Joseph make a positive first impression and certainly reflected his sense of pride in being a Hebrew.

> *Unlike Joseph during his time in prison, you probably shower (or bathe) regularly and have regular haircuts, too. So, how do you show your pride in your faith and culture? In who you are and where you come from?*

When an Opportunity Presents Itself, Go for It

There is another important lesson we can learn from Joseph's first meeting with Pharaoh.

Pharaoh has one request of Joseph: to interpret his dream. Nothing more. Nothing less. And when Joseph does exactly that, we would have expected him to stop. But he doesn't. He goes on to offer Pharaoh a plan for dealing with the seven years of famine that will ultimately come upon Egypt: "Let all the food of these good years that are coming be gathered, and let the grain be collected under Pharaoh's authority as food to be stored in the cities. Let that food be a reserve for the land for the seven years of famine which will come upon the land of Egypt, so that the land may not perish in the famine."

Wow. This may have been a good plan. It may have been the right plan. (It was!) But who is this slave, this Hebrew, to give advice to Pharaoh? Pharaoh should be angry, but he isn't. Both he and all his wise men are quite pleased with Joseph's proposal—so pleased, in fact, that Pharaoh exclaims: "Could we find another like him, a man in whom is the spirit of God?"

What can we learn from this? Quite simply, Joseph sees an opportunity. He is blessed by God with great wisdom (despite being a young man). He understands right away what to do in order to save Egypt from the terrible famine that is to come. And he can see from the faces of Pharaoh and his wise men that they are unsure how to act. Joseph therefore does not hesitate. He doesn't let his status as a slave stop him from seizing this opportunity to advise Pharaoh, and Pharaoh in turn doesn't let Joseph's status as a slave prevent him from naming Joseph ruler of all Egypt, second only to Pharaoh himself.

Is Joseph a little nervous and maybe even a little scared to give advice to Pharaoh? Possibly, but he doesn't let that stop him from seizing the opportunity before him. And, like Joseph, we should never let our nervousness (or even our feeling a little frightened) keep us from also seizing opportunities that come our way.

> *Can you remember a time when, like Joseph, you seized an opportunity? Can you remember how you overcame any feelings of nervousness or fear? Do you think others could do the same things to overcome their feelings of nervousness or fear?*

Vayigash

(Gen 44:18–47:27)

LONG TIME NO SEE

Summary of This Week's Reading

If you recall, last week's reading ended with a cliffhanger. Would Benjamin end up a slave, abandoned by his brothers, just like Joseph? Or would the brothers step forward to defend their youngest brother and by doing so make up for their actions with Joseph?

One brother does step forward: Judah. Yes, Judah, whose idea it was to sell Joseph into slavery and whose suggestion so angered the other brothers once they saw how sad Jacob was that he had to leave the family.

The truth is, since his return to the family, Judah has been the leader of the brothers. It is Judah who convinces Jacob that they need to go to Egypt to buy food. It is Judah who promises Jacob that he will keep Benjamin safe. And now it's time for Judah to fulfill that promise.

What does he do when this strange ruler of Egypt announces his intention to keep Benjamin as a slave? Judah approaches the Egyptian (never suspecting that he is really his long-lost brother Joseph) to beg for the release of Benjamin, offering to take Benjamin's place as a slave. *Judah's offer overwhelms Joseph. Memories come flooding back. His brothers, who were so cruel when they sold him as a slave, now stand ready to defend Benjamin.* "They really have changed," thinks Joseph. "They must really regret what they did to me."

It is at this point that Joseph can no longer continue with the game he has been playing. He orders all his servants to leave the room, and he stands alone before his brothers. He weeps so loudly that the servants hear him behind the closed doors. He then exclaims: "I am Joseph. Is my father still alive?"

The brothers, of course, are shocked. They cannot move. They cannot speak. Joseph sees this and understands. The brothers must be afraid that he will want revenge for what they did. Joseph tells them not to be scared or upset. He now sees that this was God's plan all along, that God sent him to Egypt so that Jacob and his brothers would have food during the years of famine.

Joseph's gentle and forgiving words convince the brothers that he speaks the truth. Joseph steps forward, kisses all his brothers, and cries. Only then are his brothers able to talk to him.

After this happy and unexpected reunion, the brothers hurry back to Canaan with the news that Joseph is alive. At first, Jacob doesn't believe them. He can't believe them. But as the brothers tell the whole story and share a message Joseph has sent him, Jacob is convinced. "Enough with the stories," he says. "My son Joseph is still alive! I must go and see him before I die."

Jacob heads down to Egypt with his wives, his sons, and all their families (70 people all together) to be reunited with his beloved Joseph after 22 years (which, by the way, is exactly how long Jacob was away from his father when he had to flee to Haran). Jacob is very excited about seeing Joseph again (who wouldn't be?), but he is also nervous. Egypt is a strange and scary country. God sees Jacob's concerns, and so He appears to Jacob in a dream. He tells Jacob not to be afraid. "I will make you there into a great nation," God promises Jacob. What's more, says God, "I Myself will go down with you to Egypt, and I Myself will also bring you back."

When Jacob arrives, he and Joseph hug and cry for a long time. Then Joseph brings some of his brothers to meet Pharaoh (it's not clear which ones). Joseph tells Pharaoh that his brothers are shepherds and *that they need many open fields for their flocks. Joseph suggests that his family be allowed to live in the fertile part of Egypt called Goshen, and Pharaoh agrees.*

This reading concludes by explaining how Joseph gathers the wealth of Egypt and how he sells food and seed during the famine. It also tells us that Jacob and his family are at this time doing quite well in their Egyptian exile.

Life Lessons from Vayigash

Seeing the Unseeable God

Joseph is one of the truly great biblical figures, so much so that the sages of the Talmud discuss and debate whether Joseph should have been the fourth of the patriarchs. Joseph is so great that he is always referred to in the Talmud as "Joseph the righteous one."

What makes Joseph so great? He is very smart. He has a special ability to interpret dreams. He is a great leader and ruler. He is strong enough in his faith that while he lives most of his life (from the age of 17 until his death at 110) in Egypt, he remains a proud Jew who believes only in God.

This is all very impressive, but perhaps Joseph's greatest attribute is his willingness to see God's hand and guiding power in every aspect of his life. Just look at what he says to his brothers once he finally tells them who he really is:

- "But now do not be sad, and let it not trouble you that you sold me here, for it was to preserve life that God sent me before you."
- "And God sent me before you to make for you a remnant in the land, and to preserve [it] for you for a great deliverance."
- "And now, you did not send me here, but God, and He made me a father to Pharaoh, a lord over all his household, and a ruler over the entire land of Egypt."

Like all great people, Joseph knows how talented he is and what he is capable of accomplishing.[1] But he doesn't give himself all the credit. He recognizes the help he gets, over and over again, from God. Joseph never thinks that sharing credit with God takes away from what he accomplishes in life. To the contrary, he understands that his accomplishments are a result of his own hard work and the grace shown him by God.

> Make a list of the ways in which you think God has blessed you and your family. Do you think you helped make these blessings happen? In what ways? Did you also show gratitude to God for these blessings? Again, in what ways?

The Importance of Forgiveness

If any individual we met in Genesis has a good reason to bear a grudge or to blame others for the events of his or her life, it's Joseph. He goes from a position of privilege as his father's favorite son to being a slave in Egypt and then spending 12 years in prison. And it's clearly his brothers' fault. They were jealous of him. They hated him. They sold him as a slave.

This is why when the brothers first discover that it's Joseph standing before them, they're shocked and can't speak. They are afraid, very afraid, that Joseph will make slaves of them all, or maybe even something worse. And what does Joseph do? He forgives them. He tells them to "please come closer to me." He hugs and kisses them, and they all cry together.

Part of the reason Joseph is so forgiving is because he realizes, as we just discussed, that God is behind this whole crazy story, which started with Joseph being sold as a slave and ends with Joseph as the ruler of Egypt in a position to save his entire family—and all of Egypt—from the famine. Still, we would have expected

---

1. Knowing that you're talented and gifted doesn't mean that you're lacking in humility. False humility would be someone like Albert Einstein saying that he wasn't very smart. True humility is admitting to yourself that anyone with the same talents and opportunities would have done as much as or more than you have.

Vayigash (Gen 44:18–47:27)

and understood if Joseph was bitter about his experiences. After all, it may have been God's plan, but in the end, it was Joseph who suffered.

In this week's reading, we have many details about Joseph's feelings and even his crying (which he seems to do a lot). These details are here to show us that Joseph's feelings of forgiveness are real and to remind us how important it is to be forgiving.

People who believe in God and trust in God usually turn to God at different times during the year to admit their mistakes and to ask for forgiveness. Some do this often; others, only occasionally. To be sure that the Jewish people take this seriously and do it regularly, the Torah even establishes a special time to seek forgiveness, from Rosh Hashanah, which marks the new year, until Yom Kippur, the Day of Atonement.

So, does this mean that God automatically forgives us, especially when we ask for forgiveness during this time of year? No, it doesn't. We have to do our part. We have to regret bad decisions or mistakes we might have made. We have to be willing to apologize to others we may have hurt. But in the end, we can't ask God to forgive us for our mistakes if we aren't willing to forgive those who have wronged us.

The story of Joseph has many lessons for us, but this one might be the most important of all!

Siblings Can Love Each Other, Too

One theme we often see repeat itself in Genesis is sibling rivalry. We have one brother who thinks about killing his brother (Esau). We have a group of brothers who openly talk about killing their brother (Joseph's brothers). We even have a brother (Cain) who actually kills his brother (Abel). Does Genesis not have anything positive to say about siblings?

Actually, it does, but you have to pay close attention to see it.

When the brothers return to Egypt and Joseph sees Benjamin for the first time, he is overcome with emotions and has to rush out of the room so that the other brothers don't see him cry. But before he leaves, he has a conversation with Benjamin. This week's reading only has a small part of that conversation, telling us that Joseph gives Benjamin a blessing. ("May God be gracious to you, my boy.") The rabbis of the Talmud give us greater insight into what these two brothers talked about. Here, according to these rabbis, is what Benjamin told Joseph:

> Joseph asked Benjamin, "Have you a brother of the same mother as yourself?"
>
> He replied, "I had a brother, but I know not where he is."
>
> "Have you sons?"
>
> He replied, "I have ten."
>
> Joseph asked him, "And what are their names?" [Benjamin goes on to tell Joseph their names.]
>
> Joseph then asked, "What is the meaning of all these names?"
>
> He replied, "They all have some reference to my brother and the troubles that have befallen him.
>
> I called one of them Bela (בלע) because he disappeared (נבלע) among foreign nations.
>
> Becher (בכר) because he was the firstborn (בכור) of our mother.
>
> Ashbel (אשבאל) because God sent him into captivity (שבאו אל).
>
> Gera (גרא) because he had to live (גר) in a foreign country.
>
> Naaman (נעמן) because he was exceedingly pleasant (נעים).
>
> Ahi (אחי) and Rosh (ראש) because he was my brother (אח) and my superior (ראש).
>
> Muppim (מופים) because he learned from the mouth (מפי) of my father.
>
> Huppim (חופים) because he did not witness my marriage (חופה —marriage canopy) and I did not witness his marriage.
>
> And Ard (ארד) because he went down (ירד) amongst the nations.

Joseph disappears and is assumed dead when Benjamin is a child, only eight or nine years old. But his relationship with Joseph is so

Vayigash (Gen 44:18–47:27)

special that Benjamin names each of his ten sons after some aspect of Joseph's life. Talk about a close and loving relationship!

Perhaps you're wondering, why doesn't Genesis include more stories like this one? Why have so many stories about brothers who don't get along? One answer is that loving relationships between siblings are the norm. It's what all parents want for their children. Sadly, siblings sometimes don't get along, and by highlighting such stories (Cain and Abel, Jacob and Esau, Joseph and his brothers), Genesis is trying to warn us about how dangerous and how unhealthy sibling rivalries can truly be.

> *Is there something that could make you love a sibling or a cousin or some other family member even more than you do? Can you imagine something that would make you not like this person? Did you ever have to ask this person for forgiveness? Did you do this on your own, or did someone else make you do it?*

Vayechi

(Gen 47:28–50:26)

ALL GOOD THINGS COME TO AN END

Summary of This Week's Reading

The final weekly reading of Genesis tells of Jacob's last years and the passing of his entire generation.

Jacob lives the final 17 years of his life in Egypt. While he may not be in the land God promised to his descendants, Jacob is very happy. He has all his sons and grandchildren with him living in comfort and safety. (It will be many years before Pharaoh makes slaves of all the Jews.)

Jacob sees and feels himself growing old, and so he asks Joseph to promise to bury him in Canaan. Jacob then blesses Joseph's two sons, Manasseh and Ephraim. Part of this blessing is that Joseph's two sons will be counted among the 12 tribes of Israel.[1]

---

1. In truth, they are counted as tribes only when it comes to getting a portion of the land of Israel. Here's how it works: The tribe of Levi gets no portion of the land. Their inheritance is to serve as priests in the holy Temple. Joseph, the favorite son, gets the double portion usually given to the firstborn son (and while he isn't the first son born to Jacob, he is the firstborn of Rachel). And so, Joseph's double portion is spilt between Manasseh and Ephraim.

Jacob then goes on to bless all his sons. He says that a tribe will be descended from each of them, and he shares with his sons the special role each tribe will have. For example, Judah will produce leaders and kings, while priests will come from Levi. Scholars will come from Issachar, and sailors from Zebulun. Teachers will come from Simeon, and soldiers from Gad. Dan will produce judges. Asher will produce olive growers.

Jacob also blesses some of his sons with special physical gifts or attributes. Naphtali is given the swiftness of a deer, and Benjamin, the ferociousness of a wolf. Joseph is blessed with beauty and is promised many descendants.

But Jacob has a long and a good memory. He scolds Reuben for moving his bed into Leah's tent after Rachel died. He is still upset with Simeon and Levi for their actions against the city of Shechem.

After Jacob dies, Joseph keeps his promise and arranges a large funeral procession to bring Jacob's body to Canaan for burial. Jacob's descendants are joined by Pharaoh's ministers, the leading citizens of Egypt, and the Egyptian cavalry. Jacob is laid to rest in the Machpelah Cave in Hebron (where Abraham and Sarah, as well as Isaac and Rebekah, are buried and where Leah will also be buried).

Like his father, Joseph dies in Egypt, at the age of 110. He, too, asks that his bones be taken out of Egypt and buried in Canaan, but this only happens when Moses takes the Jews out of Egypt many years later. Before his passing, Joseph shares with his family words of hope that will help them get through the long years of slavery that will soon come upon them: "God will surely take notice of you and bring you up from this land to the land that He promised on oath to Abraham, to Isaac, and to Jacob."

Life Lessons from Vayechi

Turning Things on Their Heads

Most of the patriarchs and matriarchs in Genesis seem young and vigorous even when they are very old. Not Jacob. He looks old and feels old, so he knows that his life will soon come to an end. He

Vayechi (Gen 47:28–50:26)

wishes to bless his sons before his death, and not surprisingly, he starts with his favorite son, Joseph. What is surprising, however, is that Jacob blesses Joseph's sons, Manasseh and Ephraim, before he blesses Joseph. And Jacob has one more surprise up his sleeve. He blesses the younger son, Ephraim, before blessing his older brother, Manasseh. In doing so, Jacob makes it very clear to Joseph that the younger brother will be the greater of the two.

This is not the first time in Genesis that the younger brother comes out on top. Abraham is the youngest of three brothers. Isaac is younger than Ishmael. Jacob is younger than Esau. And who become the leaders of Jacob's 12 sons? Not Reuven, his first born, but Judah, from whom the kings of Israel will come, and Levi, from whom the priests who serve in the Temple will come.

This pattern is so obvious that it must be here to teach us an important lesson, but what?

In the time of Genesis, most people lived in tribes, and the oldest son automatically became the leader when his father died. It didn't matter how smart or skilled this son was. The only requirement to become the leader of the tribe or of the family was to be the firstborn.

The Genesis stories of sibling rivalry come to teach us something very different. When choosing a leader, things like who is born first or who has the most money or even whose parent has the bigger or more important job don't matter so much. What really matter are the skills and talents and personality of the person being considered to become leader.

So, the next time you get to choose your class president or the captain of your school's sports teams, remember not just the story of Manasseh and Ephraim but the stories of all the brothers in Genesis. And then be sure to pick the best and most capable person for the job, not just the most popular student in your grade or class.

> *What are some character traits or skills that make a person a good leader? Is being popular one of these traits? What would you do if your best friend were running for class president and you knew that he or she was really not the best person for the job? Would you vote for your friend anyway?*

How You Feel is Not Necessarily How Others Feel

Things happen sometimes that make you feel angry or happy or sad. And when you stop and think about how you feel, you're sure that anyone would feel angry or happy or sad about the same thing or in the same circumstances.

It seems that this is exactly how Joseph's brothers think. After Jacob dies, the brothers say to themselves, "What if Joseph still bears a grudge against us? What if he wants payback for what we did to him?" They are so worried that Joseph will want revenge now that their father is dead that they make up a story, telling Joseph that Jacob spoke to them all before he died. According to the brothers, Jacob instructed Joseph to forgive his brothers.

The truth is, this is all pretty silly. Joseph has already forgiven his brothers, and Jacob's death won't change that. But the brothers aren't convinced. Maybe they don't appreciate how special and forgiving Joseph is. (If you recall, we discussed this in the previous chapter.) Maybe they think that if their situations were switched, they would want revenge on Joseph, so Joseph must feel the same way.

This is a mistake people often make. They assume their friends will think and do just as they would do. But just because you react in a certain way to something—be it a book, a movie, or a conversation among friends—doesn't mean that everyone else will react the same way.

It seems clear from the story that Joseph understands what is going on. This is why he gently and calmly speaks with his brothers and reassures them that everything is fine. He reminds them that he forgave them all a long time ago and that nothing can change that.

Here again we see that Genesis gives us a powerful example of the correct way to act. Joseph's actions remind us about the dangers of assuming other people will think or react exactly as we do.

> *Can you think of a time when you and your friends had different reactions to the same thing? Did you take the time to explain to each other how and why you felt the way you did? Looking back at this, would it have been helpful to have explained to each other how and why you felt the way you did?*

Vayechi (Gen 47:28–50:26)

A Matter of Perspective

The Jewish sages have an interesting and, some would say, very healthy outlook on life. They ask, "Who is rich?" Their answer: "The person who is satisfied with his or her portion in life." We see this attitude throughout the book of Genesis, but perhaps no more than with Jacob.

As we have discussed in the previous chapters, Jacob has a difficult life: problems with Esau and Laban, a complicated family situation, the premature death of his beloved Rachel, and the disappearance of Joseph. And these difficulties take their toll. How do we know this? When Pharaoh first meets Jacob, he is amazed at how old Jacob looks, and he asks a rather impolite question: "How old are you?" Jacob tells Pharaoh that he has yet to reach the age of his father or grandfather, and he then adds the following: "Few and hard have been the years of my life."

Is Jacob a sad person? No, quite the opposite. Tradition tells us that Jacob is very happy during his 17 years in Egypt, perhaps the happiest he has ever been in his life. He has all he could hope for, living with his children and watching his grandchildren grow. He is truly happy with his portion.

In this respect, he is not alone. Abraham and Sarah have their problems: they leave their homeland, there are famines in their new land, Sarah is kidnapped twice, and there is the whole story with Hagar and Ishmael. So, too, with Isaac and Rebekah: they have constant disputes with Abimelech and the Philistines, not to mention the running feud between Jacob and Esau. Yet, they are happy and satisfied with their portions. The Torah tells us that Abraham was blessed with all things and that Isaac was blessed from all things. In other words, they and their wives, despite whatever challenges they had, were content and happy.

But, again, it is Jacob who gives us the best example of this approach to life. If you remember, when Jacob is about to meet up with Esau after living with Laban for more than 20 years, he sends Esau many gifts. When the brothers finally greet each other face to face, Esau doesn't want to accept all the gifts Jacob sends him, because, he says, "I have a lot already." Jacob won't take no for an answer. He insists that Esau keep the gifts, because, he says, "I already have everything."

The difference between "a lot" and "everything" tells us all we need to know about how Jacob views his life.

And so, as the book of Genesis closes with the deaths of Jacob and Joseph and their entire generation, we conclude our study of their lives with this very important lesson, perhaps the most important lesson to be learned from this book:

The lives of the patriarchs and matriarchs show us that everything is a matter of perspective. They choose to focus on the positive and the blessings given them by God. Yes, their lives are sometimes challenging, but in the end, they are very satisfied with their portions, so they feel very rich.

May we all be blessed to feel so rich in our own lives.

What is the difference between having "a lot" and having "everything"? Is one better? Which one? How?

About the Author

Rabbi Reuven Travis earned his bachelor's degree from Dartmouth College, where he graduated Phi Beta Kappa, with a double major in French literature and political science. He holds a master's degree in teaching from Mercer University and also earned a master's in Judaic studies from Spertus College. He received his rabbinic ordination from Rabbi Michael J. Broyde, dean of the Atlanta Torah MiTzion Kollel, after spending four years studying with Rabbi Broyde and the members of the kollel.

    A longtime day school teacher, Rabbi Travis currently serves as the Executive Director of the College Beit Midrash of Atlanta (www.cbmatl.org). He has previously published scholarly works on the book of Job, the book of Numbers, and the book of Genesis, respectively.

www.ingramcontent.com/pod-product-compliance
Lightning Source LLC
Chambersburg PA
CBHW050835160426
43192CB00010B/2036